# Inquire Within

A Guide to Living in Spirit

James K. Papp

## Praise for *Inquire Within*

"*Inquire Within* changed my life for the better in so many ways. A series of misfortunes and loss robbed me of my joy and sense of self. I was stuck in a dark loop with no end in sight until James' book guided me on a path of self-care, spirituality, and gratitude. I've reconnected with nature and humanity on a deep and profound level. I can laugh again. By nurturing a positive mindset, I've attracted incredible opportunities and beautiful moments in my day to day life. Do yourself a kindness and read this book."
—Nikki Jefford, Author of award-winning paranormal romance novels for teens and adults
www.nikkijefford.com

"With great insight, James Papp has created a kind of 'spiritual potpourri' by carefully gleaning the essence of the world's tried and true spiritual practices. *Inquire Within* takes us right to the heart of the most important work there ever was, that of awakening. Peace, joy, compassion, and purpose are not far off. Just open the book to any page and you are likely to find just what you were looking for, presented in a way that's easy to understand and implement into daily life. Let James Papp take you by the hand and gently lead you down the path to harmony."
—Barry Dennis, Founder of Coexist Celebration and Celebration Church, author of *The Chotchky Challenge; Clearing the Clutter from your Home, Heart and Mind and Discovering the True Treasure of your Soul*
www.barryadennis.com

"*Inquire Within* is a recipe for a joyful, vibrant life. James brings light and understanding to the deepest aspects of spirit and connection, so that we can meet the world with confidence, no matter how difficult our road has been. This book has made me a better person."
—Tamara Gerlach, Author of *Cultivating Radiance: 5 Essential Elements for Holistic Self Care,*
www.tamaragerlach.com

"Healing and harmony are keys to enjoying an inspired and fulfilling life. *Inquire Within* is packed with time-tested tools to guide you there. This highly readable introduction to spiritual practice offers options for every earnest seeker. *Inquire Within* shows you that when you find balance within you are in the best position to make your own uniquely creative contribution to the world in a deep and meaningful way – a contribution that becomes all the more vital as we face not only our personal challenges but also the planetary crises of our time."
—David Christopher, Author of *The Holy Universe: A New Story of Creation for the Heart, Soul and Spirit*
www.theseekerandthe sage.com

"Your book carries a sense of calm, deep and joyful spirituality. I think it will be very beneficial to many readers."
—Curt Remington, Author of *Simple Meditation: A Spiritual Connection for Transforming Your Life,*
www.curtremington.com

"May this extraordinary book joyfully inspire, awaken, and support you with resounding grace and beauty on your spiritual journey. Aho!"
—Diana I. Falconi, Falcon Medicine Woman, www.dancemedicine.com

"Thank you so much for your book. I have begun to meditate again due to your positive influence."
—Laurie M. (reader)

"Janet and I truly enjoyed your book, extremely well written, and it came into our realm of consciousness right about the point it needed to. We both have struggled with defining religion and spirituality for ourselves. We have tried several organized religions, read many books and felt like we were just not hearing the right messages that would resonate with us. I could go on and on, but just wanted to let you know that we thank you for the book and its messages."
—Hal and Janet V. (readers)

"Jim's book couldn't have come at a better time. I was at such a low point, recovering from the challenges of alcohol abuse and in a correctional facility. I was grateful to be reminded where I come from and what I believe. Thanks again and Namasté."
—John P. (reader)

"This is an excellent guide for the beginner, as well as taking the more practiced to a deeper level. It's very readable and easy to understand. Mr. Papp's photos and poetry enliven the book. The gentle earth centered spirituality of the author shines through every page. He emphasizes that part of spiritual practice is service to others in the web of life. We are all connected. I highly recommend it."
    —Rev. Donata Ahern, Author of *The Medicine Wheel: Path of the Heart,*
    www.Donata.ChrysalisHeartCenter.com


"In recent years there has been a veritable explosion of new titles exploring the subject of spiritual development and self-awakening. And while many of these efforts would seem to have been undertaken with the best of intentions, the messages conveyed are indeed mixed and too often pedantic at best. *Inquire Within: A Guide to Living in Spirit* is a welcomed exception to this trend. Mr. Papp's words convey honesty, humility and practical encouragement. There are no shortcuts to enlightenment here. Only a renewed commitment to living a purposeful life, to sharing the Peace, Freedom and Happiness that we may discover along the Way need apply. This is a genuine guide that reminds us that the map is not the territory and that while we are certainly individuals – we can be more… Wonderful book!"
    —Eric C. (reader)

**Inquire Within: A Guide to Living in Spirit**
James K. Papp – 3rd edition

Published by: Planet Papp,
PO Box 29017, Bellingham, WA 98228-1017 USA

Copyright © 2010, 2011, 2016 James K. Papp.
All rights reserved.

No part of this book may be reproduced, stored in a retrieval system, or transmitted by any means, electronic, mechanical, photocopying, recording, or otherwise, without written permission from the publisher.

Front cover design art "Into the Garden" by Rob Schouten
All other art, photographs, and poems by James K. Papp

Printed in the United States of America

**www.inquirewithin.com**

**Publisher's Cataloging-In-Publication Data**
(Prepared by The Donohue Group, Inc.)

Names: Papp, James K., 1959-
Title: Inquire within : a guide to living in spirit / James K. Papp.
Description: 3rd edition. | Bellingham, WA : Planet Papp, [2016] | Includes bibliographical references.
Identifiers: LCCN 2016916002 | ISBN 978-0-9832041-3-8 | ISBN 978-0-9832041-4-5 (ebook)
Subjects: LCSH: Spiritual life.
Classification: LCC BL624 .P28 2016 (print) | LCC BL624 (ebook) | DDC 204/.4--dc23

A Guide to Living in Spirit 7

Lisa and James Papp

## Dedication

This book is dedicated to the memory of dear brother, David Alan Opu'ulani Burrows, and to my dear father, John Edward Papp, who taught me so much and who was truly a man of grace.

# Contents

| | | |
|---|---|---|
| Acknowledgements | | 10 |
| Foreword | | 11 |
| Preface | | 15 |
| 1. | Why Spirit Matters | 19 |
| 2. | The Altar – Creating Sacred Space | 33 |
| 3. | Offerings – The Way of Reciprocity | 45 |
| 4. | Gratitude – Being Thankful | 55 |
| 5. | Prayer – Speaking with Spirit | 65 |
| 6. | Meditation – Communing with Spirit | 79 |
| 7. | Solitude – Being with Nature | 95 |
| 8. | Fasting – A Higher Perception | 111 |
| 9. | Kindness – The Gentle Path of Joy | 119 |
| 10. | Artists of Life – Creating Inspiration | 135 |
| 11. | Ancient Wisdom – Tapping Deep Roots | 147 |
| 12. | Ceremony – Bringing It All Together | 165 |
| 13. | Living in Spirit | 175 |
| Appendix One – *Moon, Solstice, and Equinox Data* | | 179 |
| Appendix Two – *Book, Web, Music, and Movie Resources* | | 181 |
| Afterword – A Prayer | | 195 |

# Acknowledgments

I acknowledge my dear teachers for their unconditional love and support in my spiritual journey: Mary Magdalene of the Cross, Hunbatz Men, Pedro López, and Rigoberto Itzep Chanchavac of the Mayan tradition; and Diana Falconi of the Andean Q'ero tradition. To them I offer my sincerest, most heartfelt thanks.

Thank you to my dear wife and best friend Lisa Papp, for her love, for her thoughtful feedback on the manuscript, and for always believing in me. Thank you to dear sisters Maria Papp and Joni Papp, and to dear brother Roger Aldridge, for their valuable support throughout the process of making this book. With gratitude I thank Roby James for her editing excellence and Nikki Jefford for her fabulous administrative support.

I give special thanks to Donata Ahern, Lisa Aschoff, Robert Bates, Malcom Carter, David Christopher, Eric Clarke, Barry Dennis, Milo Duke, Nicholas Kirsten Honshin, Krystal Hansen-Kirsten, Birdena Leininger, Dennis Littleton, Merissa Lovett, Nancy Low, Jeni Miller, Laurie Miller, Lorraine Nay, Jamie Olson, Ray Pelley, Curt Remington, Rob Schouten, Scott Spjut, Hal Verrell, Janet Verrell, Craig Wear, and Stuart White.

And thanks to you, the reader, for joining me on my journey and inviting me into yours.

# Foreword

I've known James Papp for over 40 years. He's always had an active curiosity and wonder about our world - the outer world *and* the inner world. This curiosity about what makes life "tick" began when he was very young. In fact, James started keeping a journal when he was a child. Over the years he recorded his thoughts and epiphanies, and documented his studies and insights, particularly about Nature and spirituality.

Of all my teachers, James has been the most important to me. Through the tough times, he has stood by me. I have learned so much from his ability to look for the good in all situations, his discipline, and his kindness. I love that I am having this human experience with James, as my friend, my husband, my teacher.

James wrote this book in 2010 and continues to revise it because he wants to share new and evolving insights, particularly since the December 21, 2012 shift into the next great cycle of the Mayan calendar. He spent many years learning the culture of the Maya and I am grateful that we are sharing this spiritual exploration together, including our Mayan marriage in Mexico.

We have been deeply enriched by teachings and ceremonies with Mayan elders Hunbatz Men, in the Yucatan of Mexico, and Rigoberto Itzep Chanchavac, in the highlands of Guatemala. Closer to home, Mary Magdalene of the Cross has nourished us with her spiritual wisdom and guidance over the years. We are so grateful to these beautiful teachers for always inspiring us to live our lives in Spirit. This inspiration is woven throughout the pages of *Inquire Within*.

The Maya and many indigenous peoples around the world honor their connection with Nature and Spirit every day. This strongly draws James, who feels a reverence for Nature that began with his childhood in Alaska. The importance of our relationship with Nature as an ongoing process is a major theme he explores in this book. James and I regularly make offerings to Mother Earth and always include prayers of gratitude in our ceremonies.

Like you, I have had many life experiences. I can choose to learn and grow from those experiences and be grateful for the many gifts I have received from my family and ancestors. I have learned to see that I am so much more than my thoughts, my experiences, and my stories. I am a spiritual being having a human experience. This is another powerful theme James weaves throughout *Inquire Within* as a fundamental way to work through and move beyond being defined by one's life history and circumstances.

James and I have learned a lot about the importance of happiness. Spirit wants us to be happy. Yes, there will be challenges in life, but we can make the choice to look for the good. I haven't always been happy. My family has faced many challenges…alcoholism, abuse, divorce, and suicide. I am so grateful for the help I've had from many teachers and healers, especially James. One of the most profound teachings has been around the power of forgiveness…forgiving myself and forgiving others.

The simple, age-old practices that James outlines in this guide – such as the moving meditation of Qigong that has helped me so much – really do work. They continue to make a difference in my life and I am grateful that James has shared them in such a thoughtful book. Whether you are seeking guidance at a challenging crossroads in your life, or desiring to begin or to deepen your spiritual practice, I hope you benefit from *Inquire Within* as much as I have.

In Gratitude,

*Lisa E. Papp*

14 Inquire Within

# Preface

*The path that leads to you*
*is in my heart.*

In 1980 I was a young man with an awakening awareness. But without a roadmap or guide for my explorations I became lost and rudderless, and at one point I thought I had come to the end of my life. It was a challenging place I call the "crossroads," where I underwent what I later learned was the dark night of the soul. I turned to books to start figuring out what was happening in my life. Thankfully, spiritual authors such as Alan Watts and Ram Dass helped me understand some of what I was experiencing. I realized I was not alone, and this gave me inspiration to continue on my journey of seeking. I found myself on a track to artfully create and share positivity and light, as best I could.

In 1997 I met spiritual teacher Mary Magdalene of the Cross. As Hereditary Priestess of Temple of the Deer Wisdom School, she shared her Mayan teachings with me through ongoing lessons and initiations. Mary moved me to change my thought patterns about Spirit and about life in general, as I will explain later in the book. This was what I needed to experience life in a more harmonious and joyful way. The initiation by Mary marked my commitment to walk the path of Spirit and an acceptance of the new way I had chosen to be in the world. I began periodic pilgrimages to visit the elegant, time-stoppingly magical Mayan temples in Mesoamerica.

In 2005 I was again at a crossroads. This time I seriously needed to heal my past and rebalance my lifestyle in order to continue on my path. I was greatly stressed and had to admit I was unhappy. This was a crushing blow to my ego. But I knew I had to help myself; if I didn't do it, no one else would. So I went looking for a healer. I was blessed to meet Falcon Medicine Woman Diana Falconi.

Diana's shamanic healings were extremely effective and she inspired me to work, under her guidance, with the medicine wheel in the context of her Andean Q'ero lineage. I devoured teachings on the energy medicine of the Americas, learned a deeper value of ceremony, and devoted myself fully to living in Spirit.

Leading up to 21 December 2012, a huge amount of doomsday negativity and misinformation circulated about what this important Mayan calendar date really meant. I wanted to write about what the Mayans themselves had to say, as their voices weren't getting much attention. However, teacher Mary burst my bubble by advising me that sharing more Mayan prophesy was not what people needed. If I wanted to write, she counseled, then I should write about what we are really looking for underneath our worries – how to live a fearless, harmony-filled life that is led by Spirit. And so I began the process of making this book. All along the way I have been blessed by my partnership with my wife and chief collaborator, Lisa.

In the pages ahead I share what I have learned about a variety of time-tested tools you can use to live in a more spiritually conscious manner. These practical spiritual technologies help us connect more fully with our source, that we may come into harmony with the universal cosmic energies which inform all of existence and power our being. Our lives are underpowered and incomplete when we are unaware of the ultimate source of our power.

I feel great gratitude for all who have inspired me. My teachers shine as beacons of light to so many, guiding and reminding all around them to live in Spirit with kindness and with respect for all life. This book is my humble attempt to follow in their tradition of sharing. I wish you many blessings on your path.

*James K. Papp*

18  Inquire Within

## Chapter One

# Why Spirit Matters

*The great journey
is there for all of us.
Waiting in the shade
under a tree
by the bend in the road,
it calls on us
to journey higher,
to the trail that points
into the very Heart of Heaven.*

Who am I? Why am I here? What is the meaning of life? What is happening to me, and how can I be truly happy? When we sit in silence and ask the great questions, something mysterious and magical begins to happen. The answers come to us as a calling that takes us within, to our inner temple – a place of infinite love and possibility. Here, where Spirit's presence may be revealed, is where our great journey begins, even if we don't know we're on a great journey until it surfaces in our lives. This is where we find ourselves living in Spirit.

Living in Spirit we regain our balance, find our center, and come into tune with the totality of ourselves as beautiful instruments in the grand symphony of existence. Here we experience peace, joy, and even ecstasy, and we feel a profound sense of contentment – liberating foundations of a rich and creatively satisfying life.

It is truly wonderful when our life journey is going well and everything is running smoothly. But what about when things are not working well for us? Sometimes we're happy with our partner, happy with our livelihood and with where we live, yet we feel a general dissatisfaction with life that we don't understand and cannot shake. Most of us, sooner or later, find ourselves at a crossroads in life where we are out of balance, not sure what to do or which way to go. Without a roadmap or guide we can become lost and rudderless. We might even throw up our hands, exclaiming we don't have enough information or insight or energy, and we need help in order to continue on our journey.

Many life conditions may bring us to the crossroads. Depression, addiction, divorce, an accident, the death of a loved one, the loss of a job, imprisonment, or just too much stress – these are some of the situations which can leave us feeling drained of energy and powerless, without inspiration or direction. And beyond the immediate shock of the experience at hand, we are dismayed, angered, or demoralized by not being able to jump start or heal our own lives. We want to be self-sufficient and able to right our own ship on the ocean of life. We can visit the crossroads periodically, even in little ways, like when we lose our cool and behave outside our integrity.

Crossroads

We are raised in the modern world with independence as the goal. Yet the connections we share are vital. It is our connections with others which create the community where our basic needs are met and where we can develop our individuality and shine brightly - for our own benefit and for the benefit of all. We take turns helping each other as we progress through the crossroads of life. At times a seriously challenging place, the crossroads offers us great opportunity for personal growth and transformation.

We have to be aware that we can find drama all around us at the crossroads, and as we encounter the twists and turns and ups and downs in life. But we do not have to engage in drama – especially negative or powerless drama. We only need to know one thing: how to live. Spirit leads us there.

There is a big difference in living between surviving and thriving. Once I went to a meditation center in San Diego. After the meditation, someone asked whether it really mattered if one works consciously to improve their life. The minister was silent for a moment and then gave the following reply: if you work on your life, and are actively involved in your personal growth, changes will happen and you will evolve. And if you don't work on your life and just let it go, then change – probably more difficult change – will happen and eventually you will evolve. It is really a matter of what type of life experience you want to have. And there is another viewpoint to consider. If we do not make the effort to work on our lives, we may stagnate or even devolve.

There are two approaches to engage with on one's life cycle: more awake or less awake. We have the capacity to help ourselves or to hurt ourselves. We can go with the flow, in tune with universal energy, or we can go against the flow. In the long run we get out of life what we put into it. Again, it is really a matter of what type of life experience you want to have. And ultimately it is about taking responsibility for one's life.

*Stretch (a bow) to the very full,
And you will wish you had stopped in time.*[1]

~ *Laotse*

Your choices in life are not just about what you want to have. Your choices are also about how you want to be and what you are manifesting by your way of being in the world. At every moment you have an opportunity to become more aware of how you carry yourself – what you are thinking about and what is motivating you. How we perceive life, through our habits, assumptions, and attitudes, colors our life experience. So, you can ask yourself: How do I choose to perceive the process of life – the ongoing, energetic, all-encompassing act of living in the world? Your answer to this question is critical because energy cannot help but follow thought. Whatever you focus on becomes real. In fact, every single thing in your life is at stake.[2]

Spiritually, all roads, all life paths walked on this Earth, ultimately lead to the same destination, to the same unity in Spirit. So the real question is, what type of life do you want to experience along the way? How do you want to feel? How do you really want to live?

Think about your life, your city, your society, your world, your relationships. What are you experiencing at this moment? What do you really want to be experiencing deep

---

[1] Edited by Lin Yutang, The Wisdom of Laotse (New York, Random House, 1948).

[2] Joni Papp (conversation with author, 2009).

down inside? Energy follows thought, so what do you want to manifest?

All of the variables in our lives – our spouses, our lovers, our friends, our homes, our possessions, our jobs, our bodies, our everything – are changing and transitory, always in flux. Even our souls, as reservoirs of experience across this life and all lifetimes, clearly change. Everything changes; nothing stays the same – except Spirit. Spirit is the one thing in our lives which appears constant, consistent, and always enduring. We can always count on it to be here for us. (Spirit is infinite, yet who knows, maybe Spirit is growing and changing, too!)

What exactly is Spirit? In the simplest terms, Spirit is the energy of awareness and consciousness. To some it is what made consciousness. It is the intelligence and love underlying all existence. Spirit is that which is not dependent on anything – not form, not time, not circumstances. Spirit simply *Is*, always in the present. When we are present in the here and now, then we are in resonance with the entire Universe – a condition which can spontaneously generate feelings of joy, happiness, and ecstasy; and feelings of gratitude, appreciation, and peace. Being present is where the great path of healing begins and where we will always find it when we need to look for it. When we find ourselves at a crossroads in life, our first task is simply to be present. Knowing this, what is the benefit of keeping a spiritual practice? Why try to add yet one more thing to our already busy days when we don't seem to have enough time as it is? Will it really help? These are good questions. Here is a simple answer.

**Spiritual practice is our individualized way of learning to live in the ever-present now.** When we are living in the present, we are living in Spirit.

**Living in Spirit provides a rudder which guides us in seas both smooth and stormy.** A spiritual practice gives us a compass by which to navigate our lives. It brings us into the present, where healing occurs and where joy resides. Spirit is the one thing which is always there for us, regardless of the state of all the variables in our lives. A spiritual practice helps us awaken to who we really are. It moves us in the direction of awareness, of trust in the process of life, and of our own intuitive knowing. It helps us realize that our inner value is not at all dependent upon our life conditions or circumstances. A spiritual practice can put us on a course which generates compassion, peace, and love – building self-esteem and bringing many blessings to ourselves and to all beings.

**The ultimate aim of a spiritual practice is to "know thyself," to remember who and what we are, and to experience one's own divinity - in other words, to *know* that one is an eternal, radiant soul of pure Spirit.**

> *We are not human beings having a spiritual experience.*
> *We are spiritual beings having a human experience.*[3]
>
> *~ Pierre Teilhard de Chardin*

---

[3] Pierre Teilhard de Chardin (French philosopher, priest, paleontologist, and geologist ca. 1881-1955 AD).

Most of us, to one degree or another, have lost the awareness of the original essence of our being. We are out of touch with the wellspring of unencumbered vitality and joy that has always been within us. Because of this, we no longer feel our connection with Spirit and with the Earth. We are asleep and no longer know, feel, or remember that all of us on this Earth are one family of brothers and sisters. This includes not only human beings, but all the animals and plants, as well. It is as if we are under an anesthetic.

We have become anesthetized by many things – by power, by greed, by governments and corporations, by TV and the media, by our diets, by abuse of alcohol and drugs and, most of all, by our own minds. We fabricate a continual stream of thoughts: judgments about the past and worries about the future. Add to that news stories on war, violence, and economic disaster, and we are deluged by despair caused by the ignorance of our interconnectedness.

Our hearts and minds are obscured by all those things which mask our original instincts, the natural knowing which is inherent in all of us. As a result we are not adequately able to feel the consequences of our actions. In this modern, civilized world we have become numb. We have lost the awareness of our very spiritual and super-energetic connection with all that is. In what often seems like a materialistic world, the way forward is not by denying the material but rather by making room for the spiritual as we live each day.

**Putting Spirit first sets the table for the rest of your life.** A commitment to spiritual practice places you in a favorable position as you undergo your life journey. It enhances your connections with other people and the environment around and within you. It helps you appreciate what you have in life and to have compassion for what others are going through in their lives. Recognizing that Spirit is primary will teach you to see all your assets and hopes – as well as your issues and challenges – in a light which allows you to accept them and work with them instead of being controlled by them. This leads to harmonious balance and a confident calmness in life, bringing joy and peace to yourself and to all you share your life with.

For many years, as a young man, I wanted to have a spiritual practice. I tried meditation and yoga, but without a teacher or training, I was too unsettled to commit to them (and perhaps I didn't know how to commit). I dabbled, moving in and out of various techniques, none of which stayed with me. Then at a critical point, when my life was in such disarray and disharmony, I found myself practicing meditation and prayer because I *needed* to. With my newfound focus and determination, I began to find my center.

Committing to a spiritual practice can be hard. So, dear reader, regardless of the space you may find yourself in, do not be discouraged. It is okay and even natural if the beginning of one's spiritual practice is caused by discomfort or unhappiness. Discomfort is a potential opportunity and can be a powerful, energizing force for positive change in our lives, as it wakes us up. No matter your life situation, there is hope!

> *A feeling I know*
> *a feeling I have had before,*
> *arriving at the border*
> *of the unknown,*
> *where the air is charged*
> *and the sun casts*
> *black shadows,*
> *where the sky surrounds*
> *and the earth curves away.*

*It is a moment*
*and it is timeless,*
*a pause pregnant*
*with every possibility.*
*It is the gate*
*of life and death,*
*a place where*
*reunion with the eternal*
*part of oneself awaits.*
*A shiver ripples*
*up my spine and I know*
*I must step forward*
*through the door.*
*A deep breath…*
*and I step forward*
*on the path.*

The belief that spiritual practice is full of ease and light and doesn't require us to do work is a fallacy. Continuing on a spiritual path brings up challenges and blockages as the seasons of our lives cycle through. This is one of Spirit's ways of causing us to grow. We succeed by expanding and becoming larger than our problems – meeting them head on with open arms, open hearts, and open minds, and not trying to avoid them. Maybe that is why it's called a practice! Yet if we proceed at whatever speed is comfortable for each of us on our paths, doing what we can when we are able to, with heartfelt intent, it will inevitably lead to evolution and growth.

As we cultivate harmony through living in Spirit we become in tune with ourselves and generate peace in our lives. This gives us momentum, energy, and confidence on our path – a spiritual gyroscope which works to maintain balance through the many changes, twists, and turns of living. We can now accept and even embrace all the events of life which we formerly viewed as negative or disastrous and we can cease judging ourselves and others so intensely.

We begin to see there is a harmonious design to our lives and that everything happens for a reason. Challenges and lessons still appear, but now we are working *with* the flow of energy – not against it. We get out of our own way, enabling ourselves to accept unpredictability and change, without all the stress and anxiety that comes with it. We are progressively transforming ourselves – our minds, our emotions, even our physical bodies – to operate at higher levels. Through this spiritual alchemy, we become peaceful, and we learn how to live. Joy is now with us on our path of discovery – a path which becomes no less than the epic journey of the heart.

Enlightenment, peace, fulfillment – whatever you want to call it – is not some faraway, pie-in-the-sky, seemingly unattainable thing. It is here in every moment. We can access it through simple practices and unassuming ways. The tried-and-true spiritual technologies developed and carried forward by our ancestors over the millennia are not only here for us in times of need but function as part of our daily lives. We may find our center and live within it to be nourished by our own wholeness.

This wholeness we are looking for is found within, in patience and acceptance. It is found in non-judgment and in the unspeakably vast spaces of communion opened up by vehicles such as prayer, meditation, gratitude, and kindness. We find the way when we take responsibility for ourselves and exercise the great courage it takes to be who we really are.

**Healing is being who you really are.**

Here are a few notes to keep in mind as you read ahead. First, when I speak of Spirit, please feel free to exchange the word Spirit with God, the Universe, the Source, Life Force, Light, Love, Ultimate Reality, the Great Mother, the Divine, or whatever name represents for you the creative cosmic energy which causes and includes everything that exists.[4]

Second, a spiritual practice does not exclude practicing a formal religion, but what we are focusing on here is practicing spirituality – inviting Spirit into one's life and working with it as a conscious, consistent, ongoing process.

Third, practice is the process which transforms our intent into results.

Lastly, each of us begins our path from where we are and proceeds at our own speed in our own way; none of us is judged. There is nothing to fear.

The following passage is by the great spiritual teacher Paramahansa Yogananda in his book *Journey to Self-Realization: Discovering the Gifts of the Soul*. I share this with you, as it speaks profoundly about the value of spiritual practice:

> *It is an insult to your Self to be born, live, and die without knowing the answer to the mystery of why you were sent here as a human being in the first*

---

[4] I am necessarily using words to talk about that which cannot be named or described (the unnameable One). We have to work past the duality of talking about us and God. For Spirit is All, and we are part of that All – All is who we are. We are the circle of life and nothing is outside it.

*place. To forget God is to miss the whole point of existence. Learn to feel God, and to enjoy Him. Make it a habit and you will see in time how much you have gained. Acquiring material possessions and prosperity is no safeguard against sorrow. There will come a day when you will feel totally helpless, a mere pawn of destiny; and then you will begin to realize that God alone is your haven of security. He doesn't want to impose Himself on anyone. You must take the initiative to seek Him through your own fervent desire, preferring Him to all other desires. As the swan can swim through muddy waters with its feathers remaining unsoiled, so should you live in this world. If you coat your mind with the oil of nonattachment, then material desires cannot cling to you.*[5]

---

[5] Paramahansa Yogananda, *Journey to Self-Realization: Discovering the Gifts of the Soul* (Los Angeles, Self-Realization Fellowship, 1997) - reprinted with permission of Self-Realization Fellowship.

## 32 Inquire Within

*Chapter Two*

# The Altar – Creating Sacred Space

*Home for a drink of water
between lifetimes.*

Sometimes I am asked where to start when people are ready to make Spirit a more important part of their life. This happens most often when they are going through significant life changes or challenges. Usually the first thing I suggest they do is to make an altar.

Traditionally, an altar is a physical structure upon which sacrifices or other offerings are made for spiritual purposes. An altar is also a sacred place where ritual ceremonies take place. Altars are the central and most important part of the temples, shrines, and sacred places of all spiritual cultures around the world. They have been used for tens of thousands of years.

As Spirit is omnipresent, every place is sacred, so an altar can be perceived anywhere. An altar can be a mountain vista at sunrise or a rock looking out over the endless sea. Typically, it is a physical place which invites us to connect and commune with Spirit. For our purposes here we are talking about creating a sacred space for personalized exploration and practice.

Mythologist Joseph Campbell described sacred space as a place where wonder can be revealed. He considered having one's own sacred space to be an absolute necessity in this day and age. He said you need a place where you don't know what the news of the day is, what you owe anybody, or what they owe you. A personal sacred space is simply a place where you can be, creatively incubate, and become.[6]

The Q'ero – a Quechua community of people living high in the Andes mountains of Peru – carry portable altars called *mesas*. Alberto Villoldo, a shaman (or healer) trained in this tradition, describes the *mesa* as "a collection of power objects through which one engages the forces of Nature," which is also the center of ritual.[7] This is an appropriate way to think about the power an altar has as an interface, intermediary, or conduit to connect and work with the world of Spirit.

---

[6] Joseph Campbell, with Bill Moyers, *The Power of Myth* (New York, Doubleday, 1988).

[7] Alberto Villoldo, with Erik Jendresen, *Dance of the Four Winds* (Harper & Row, 1990).

## The Altar – Creating Sacred Space

For your personal workings, an altar functions foremost as a declaration that you have made Spirit a priority in your life. It is like a spiritual kitchen where recipe (your intent) and ingredients (your practices) are merged together in spiritual alchemy. An altar is also an antenna to help you focus your attention on the finer cosmic energies available when awareness and awakening are cultivated in your life. Further, an altar serves as a reminder to keep your mind turned toward Spirit. We can forget or we get busy and don't seem to have time to slow down. Both anchor and inspiration, altars help to root and center us, and to awaken and propel us toward the memory and realization of our divine nature.

**While all the Earth's places are sacred, making your own altar creates a defined, personal sacred space just for you.** Your altar becomes a safe place, your own personal sanctuary, and a place of power suitable for ceremony, prayer, meditation, or simply finding peace in your life. Spiritual practice – and the overall practice of living a spiritual life – begins with creating sacred space, centering yourself within the four cardinal directions, with heaven above and earth below.

The first altar I spent time around was a Buddhist altar at a friend's house when I was in my 20s. My friends would be chanting these beautiful, glorious, rich, golden tones, ringing their Nepalese bell, and I loved the peacefulness of the space they had created for themselves. Being there felt good, whether the altar was in use or not. It seemed to emanate serenity. Later, when I became serious about having a spiritual practice, it seemed logical to me that having an altar would be a central part of it.

My altar grew as a collage of different spiritual influences over time, rather than from following any specific religious lineage. Whatever objects inspired me particularly deeply became part of the altar. Some of these items have changed over the years, and others have remained and grown more meaningful to me along the way.

Initially my altar was made to create a quiet space where I could be unbothered to practice meditation. I had wanted to meditate for several years, but did not have the focus until I made a place for it. Sitting in my little space in front of the altar instantly calmed me which allowed the ease and peace of mind for meditation to take root and grow.

Now, every morning upon awakening, I stand in front of the altar, light a candle, and say this prayer.

> *Good morning and welcome to this day...*
> *Oh Great Spirit, Oh Father Sun, Oh Mother Earth:*
> *Thank you for this day*
> *Thank you for this life*
> *Thank you for this body temple*
> *Thank you for this soul of pure Spirit*
> *Thank you for these dear companions*
> *Thank you for this wonderful, magical, beautiful, mysterious world we share together.*
> *I am so grateful for this life and all that is in it.*
> *Thank you, thank you, thank you,*
> *thank you, thank you,*
> *I am so very blessed.*
> *Thank you for your directions*
> *which create the sacred space of our lives*
> *and guide us...*
> *Thank you, thank you, thank you...*

I acknowledge and thank the four directions as I turn to them. Then I thank Mother Earth below, Father Sun and Great Spirit above, and the center, infinite place of healing and renewal. This prepares me for meditation. I sit on a pillow on the floor in front of the altar, and it feels good just to sit there, just to be.

Before the altar everything else in my life becomes secondary. Sure, I still have thoughts occurring in my mind; maybe I'm thinking about my job or something I need to do. I notice what's in my mind, and it tells me what is happening in my life – what is concentrating itself on me and what I am concentrating on. But it's really just about being, about neutrally acknowledging whatever state I am in, hanging out calmly in the present, not forcing anything.

I love sitting there, candle glowing, communing with Spirit. Some mornings – maybe on a New Moon or the birthday of a loved one or a day of remembrance for someone departed – I'll light a stick of incense and watch its smoke curlicue and rise into the air – slowly, subtly filling the space, sanctifying it further. This causes me even more relaxation and comfort in this place I have made to honor Spirit and to honor myself.

A deep feeling of satisfaction and relaxation comes with this daily routine. When I travel or I am out in Nature with the great altar of the Universe before me, my *mesa* – my portable altar bundled in cloth – accompanies me.

Altars, indoor and out

**To make an altar, select a place for it in your abode.** Maybe it is an extra room or perhaps it is one side or a corner of a room with other uses. Ideally, select a table, cabinet, or some other piece of furniture to build your altar upon. If you are short on space, it can even be made on a shelf or windowsill, but it should be someplace dedicated only to this purpose which can remain uncluttered. Avoid it being beside a TV or whatever may be a distraction for you.

If you can, burn sage in the space prior to making your altar, and definitely thoroughly dust and clean the entire area. This clears the space of any old or unwanted energy which has accumulated there. Purifying your space also honors it and sets up an appropriate field for Spirit to work its magic. It is important to have a clean start for this important new beginning in your life.

Once you have set up your physical space, you might cover your altar surface with a nice piece of fabric. Originally, I used colorful placemats or napkins. Eventually I found beautifully woven fabrics from a place in Mexico which inspires me. Weavings such as these connect us with our ancient ancestors and, as symbols of harmony, represent the interconnected web of life. The idea is to decorate the altar, making it special for you while honoring it and protecting it.

Next, place the items of importance to you upon your altar. You can use stones, crystals, candles, incense burners, flowers, shells, feathers, or any object which feels right to you. A single simple object has the capacity to harmonize you and turn your attention toward Spirit. Candles are commonly found on altars. These artifacts can become your personal objects of power, if they are not so already. Together they create a mood, help you focus, calm you and, at the same time, inspire you. Lay out your power objects in a deliberate, ritual manner, with a sense of order to demonstrate harmony and intent.

Objects that you have a special feeling for become imbued over time with what the Maya call *Ch'ulel,* or soul essence.[8] By repeated use they are venerated and become living objects of power with inner souls, directly related to the holiness and

---

[8] David Freidel, Linda Schele, Joy Parker, *Maya Cosmos, Three Thousand Years on the Shaman's Path* (New York, William Morrow and Company, 1995).

divinity of your own soul. You may wish to take care by limiting who else, if anyone, handles them.

A pillow will make your altar space more comfortable to sit in, or select a special chair if that is better for you. Ask yourself what images, shapes, and colors turn your mind toward Spirit. Decorating your space with inspiring pictures will add to its ambiance. Images of Nature scenes, inspirational teachers, and spiritual art are options to consider. Creating a vision board for your sacred space is an empowering experience. In the art chapter we will discuss vision boards.

You might enjoy a bell or a small singing bowl, cut greens or flowers, or perhaps a piece of fruit to place on your altar as an offering. If you have affirmations you like, you can write them on cards to page through, recite or contemplate while you sit. Some people enjoy listening to music in their sacred space.

Consider in what direction you orient your altar. Maybe a certain orientation inspires you more. I like facing the east, the direction of the morning sunrise. Some use the ancient Chinese system of *Feng Shui* to orient their altar and to lay out their objects upon it. The most important thing is to create a place that inspires you, that makes you want to be in it and causes you to think of Spirit, of beauty, of mystery. Let it be a magnetizing space that pulls you in and attracts you to easily spend quality time there.

After sitting for a while at your altar and noticing the thoughts rattling around in your head, you begin to calm down. It can feel so good just to sit! You are then in a good space for praying or meditating. You may hear a far-off sound – a car on a distant street or a bird call outside the window. In this peaceful space, listen to the sound of silence, notice your breath, and relax further. Do not keep track of time. Give yourself permission to do nothing. This is about being.

In my practice, after I have sat for a while and settled down, my focus turns to communing with Spirit. I think or say, "Great Spirit, I am here, I am here, I am here" announcing my presence and stating I am conscious of what I am doing and that I am intending communion. I may say a prayer, such as:

> *Oh Great Spirit, Dear God,*
> *Thou who moveth me*
> *Thou who moveth the Earth and all the Heavens*
> *Thou who is That I Am,*
> *Thou who illuminateth my soul*
> *Thou who filleth my mind with good thoughts*
> *And my heart with the lilt of joy*
> *Thou who is That I Am,*
> *I love you*
> *I thank you*
> *I am one with you always*
> *In the Temple of Infinite Spirit.*
> *Aum, Peace, Amen.*

**We have to make an effort in order to keep continuing on our path.** Spiritual practice is about being, but it is also about going further and consciously committing to the evolutionary, transformational journey of the soul. For as long as we are here on this Earth, we are still learning. We are always moving deeper into that union, through communion. For me, working with an altar refocuses me and helps me move along my path. It is a precious activity I honor, respect, and would not want to miss out on.

To finish my morning routine, I stand, touch the palms of my hands together in a prayer pose, and declare "May the Blessings Be! Everything is as it should be."[9] I open arms wide, stretch them upward, and affirm quietly, "I love this life." This thankfulness and gratitude emanates into the entire universe, outwardly and within, placing me in a harmonious relationship with living and setting the tone for my day.

**The altar serves as a powerful organizing force.** It declares your readiness and willingness to live in Spirit. It is a Spirit attractor – even while Spirit is with us at every moment in every place. An altar creates a safe space where your practice can form and rain upon you its many blessings. It can create peace in your home and order in your life.

When you have made your altar, you will have your own personal place of power - a place where you can meditate, contemplate, pray, or do whatever constitutes for you the core of your spiritual practice. Your altar is like a miniature sacred site. There you can study and explore, commune with Spirit, and observe and get to know yourself more. An altar gives you a space to contemplate how you are experiencing life and how you *want* to experience life. Your altar grounds you and inspires you.

---

[9] Mary Magdalene of the Cross (Temple of the Deer Wisdom School).

# The Altar – Creating Sacred Space

**Altars - Three Tips:**

1. Start simply. Even a single candle set gracefully upon a small, bare table with the right intention can create a powerful sacred space.

2. Spend at least fifteen minutes a day with your altar, where you are entirely present with nothing else requiring your attention. This will help you build your relationship with it so you can benefit more from it. It will also build your confidence in the process. Later, increase your time to twenty or thirty minutes a day.

3. Carry a stone, shell, or other object of power with you during your day – something that will remind you of Spirit. Put it in a pocket or in your purse, perhaps within a small drawstring or zippered bag. Or wear it around your neck.

**Altars – Key Words:** Antenna, Center, Temple, Safe Space, Reminder

## Chapter Three

# Offerings – The Way of Reciprocity

> *Green of greens*
> *purple of purples,*
> *speak to me*
> *in the language of my heart.*

Lighting a candle is a symbolic act. It signifies light overcoming darkness and awareness overcoming ignorance, fitting metaphors for our journey on a spiritual path. It is the illumination of truth in the process of remembering who we really are. Lighting a candle or a stick of incense is also an offering and an invitation to Spirit. It says, "Here we are in this sacred space together; be with me."

Traditionally, an offering is the sacrifice of a plant, animal, or human life, the giving of blood, or a sacrifice of a precious object for religious purposes. An offering can also be a devotional practice, a tithe, or a donation. On a grander scale, it can be a dedication of one's life to a cause or even to Spirit.

**Giving something of value is the essence of making an offering.** As nothing is more valuable than life itself, our ancestors would ritually kill an animal – a chicken, for example – as part of a ceremony important enough to warrant that degree of sacrifice. The practice of animal sacrifice still occurs in some parts of the world today.

However, we no longer need to act in such an extreme manner. Lighting a stick of incense or placing a flower upon your altar can be an entirely effective offering when done with genuine intent. These acts acknowledge your desire to be with Spirit. Like a sign, it says to Spirit, "I am open for your business." A burning candle is symbolic of God's eternal light and the reality that everything in existence is made of energy. As such, a candle is the most basic, core object to be found on altars in virtually all cultures around the world.

Placing a piece of fruit on your altar is the giving up of precious food – a sacrifice – which also nourishes and sustains Spirit. It says, "Spirit, take this food; I need it for my body to live, but my soul needs you as much as my body needs food. Thank you, thank you, thank you."

**Make offerings when you are quiet, when you are fully present, and let the moment guide you in prayer or ceremony to amplify your offerings.** Sincerity and intention are powerful magnifiers of your action and you can use them to empower your offerings.

# Offerings – The Way of Reciprocity

Why not make an offering at the place you live now, which supports you and sustains you? Even if you are going to leave that place and move on, an offering can help you leave it with gratitude, and you will have a clearer transition to your new home.

Offerings are great for traveling. As the entire world is sacred, there is no limit to the places we can make them. Examples of offerings that can be made "on the road" are burying a stone on the land you grew up on or at a mountain or lake which inspires you, or leaving something of value at a place you love to be or to which you want to return to.

When traveling through the wilderness or to some place which calls to you, take along a stone of special value to you with the express purpose of giving it to Mother Earth or to Great Spirit as an offering. The act of giving the stone then becomes a physical prayer – a prayer which can serve many purposes. It can be a prayer for safe passage. It can be an offering to acknowledge the great feeling of gratitude you have for being in a place of beauty and splendor. Or it can be an offering expressing sheer gratitude for simply being alive. Be creative.

There are many reasons offerings are made and many ways to make them. The *Sherpas* of Nepal hold ceremonies before guiding climbers into the great mountains of the Himalaya – burning incense, flying prayer flags, and praying for the safety of all in the climb.

One summer before I spent two weeks hiking in the mountains, I selected two pieces of quartz to take along as offerings. I did not know when or where I would give these two rocks back to the Earth. I just carried them with me, knowing the right place would eventually reveal itself.

48    Inquire Within

Quartz stone offerings

About a week into the hike, I came to a beautiful alpine lake. Some clouds started forming above the pass I had to cross, so I stopped to analyze the weather. Soon thunder started and I realized this was the time and place to make the offering.

After acknowledging the directions, I made a prayer of thankfulness for all the wonderful blessings of this life and the great gratitude I felt for being in this fantastic place. I asked for safe passage, for protection on this journey and always, and that I might return safely home to my dear wife. I asked Mother Earth to please accept the offering and threw the first of the stones into the lake, making my prayer that much more meaningful, for we are just temporary caretakers of anything physical we have in this life. We do not own anything here. I then made a prayer for my dear companion, that she too might have safe passage on her journey in this life, and I threw the second stone into the lake.

Some years ago, I buried my biggest and best crystal in the Earth at a time Lisa and I were looking to buy our first house. We hiked up on a bluff above Puget Sound to a place special to us, and I "installed" the crystal generator as a sort of homing beacon toward our city and the morning sun. It was carefully dressed in two beautiful cloths, wrapped with a ribbon, and buried as a sacrificial tool to help guide us to our new home and our new life. Filled with accumulated energy and intent, the crystal had become an ambassador in attracting more positive energy into my life. Five months later we moved into our new house.

**The way of reciprocity in the *Q'ero* Andean tradition is called *Ayni*, and is the central principle governing their ways of life.**[10] Reciprocity means mutual exchange. In Q'ero culture, periodic acts of reciprocity are required in order to keep balance in one's life and in the life of the family and the village. In this context, reciprocity is a continued practice of making offerings that give thanks for all that has been given to us, and to ensure that we will continue receiving the support and sustenance we need from the Universe. Ceremonies ranging from simple to elaborate are performed to this end. The concept of giving back and of honoring Mother Earth, Father Sun, and Great Spirit makes a lot of sense; our ancestors' practice of making offerings is an established way to regain and maintain harmony.

---

[10] J.E. Williams, *The Andean Codex* , Adventures and Initiations Among the Peruvian Shamans (Charlottesville, Hampton Roads Publishing Company, 2005).

*All peoples acknowledge
the Great Creator.*

~ *Yakama Nation*[11]

Offerings can be made in many places in Nature: in the ocean, in a lake or river, on a mountain, in the desert sands, down in the roots of a tree, or buried in the Earth. There are no limits. You need only be guided by your imagination and a desire to reciprocate for what you have received in this life. There are traditions where tobacco, wine, or other alcohol is ritually spilled upon the Earth, given to Her in gratitude before its consumption or as part of a ceremony. Even giving a little drinking water to the Earth can be a worthwhile offering.

Offerings at home can be made in your yard, on your altar, at a nearby park, or wherever you are inspired to make them. There are no rules, except to be guided by good intention. The act of making the offering amplifies your intent. This is a way to elevate a wish or a prayer, a way to give back to Spirit or to the Earth, and a method of giving thanks for your life and all that has been has given to you.

I sometimes leave little stones or crystals on outside windowsills, on top of light fixtures, or in other unsuspected places in houses or hotels I have appreciated. After I place them, I wonder if they will ever be noticed and, if they are, what the responses may be. Maybe they will be a nice surprise for someone.

---

[11] Yakama Nation Cultural Museum, quotation displayed, Toppenish.

## Offerings – The Way of Reciprocity

A crystal later buried in the Earth

When possible, revisit the places where you made an offering. Reflect on the original intention of the offering. Note what has passed since then and feel gratitude for it. This strengthens connection with the place and adds value to the offering.

The first time I went to the Mayalands in Mexico, I was very excited. The centerpiece of my visit was a pilgrimage to Yaxchilan, a remote and ancient Mayan city deep in the jungle of Chiapas. I brought with me a special stone – a palm-sized piece of half-polished, beautiful green jade; I knew jade was highly valued by the Maya. The following is an entry from my journal at Yaxchilan:

*Aahh! The lost world of harmony is before mine eyes…through the plaza, past stelae, up the hill to Temple 33, and way up on the hill on a path to Temple 41. Climbing to the top of Temple 41 one sees forever in all directions. I am elated! I say my prayers. To the east I bless this house. To the north I bless this space. To the west I bless this marriage. To the south I bless this face. I pray to the south and the sun that I may be blessed to be the good husband, the good father, and the good artist who will bring love, light, hope, happiness, and harmony to our earthly family. Then I throw my beautiful jade offering far and deep down the hill into the jungle below. My mission is accomplished. I am complete, renewed. My vision is before me, clear and bright. I love this life. I am so thankful for everything. Evam maya e ma ho!*[12] *Amen.*

I encourage you to make your own pilgrimage, with your own offering, to a place of special meaning to you. It may be a place from your past which needs honoring, healing, or thanking. It may be a place in your future which calls to you. Or it may be right at home, if that is where your attention is drawn. Do it on whatever scale and in whatever way is appropriate for you. The entire process of planning and undertaking the journey becomes a ceremony which will give you satisfaction, joy, and confidence on your path. In a way you, yourself, will become the offering.

---

[12] José Argüelles, *The Mayan Factor, Path Beyond Technology* (Santa Fe, Bear & Company, 1987). *Evam maya e ma ho!* means "All Hail the Harmony of Mind and Nature!"

**Offerings - Three Tips:**

1. Be on the lookout and collect ahead of time items to be used for offerings. Then, when you are moved to make an offering, you have some objects handy to choose from.

2. To make a really powerful offering, give up an object of greater value to you. This will more effectively energize and activate what you are working on.

3. Be creative and go with your gut instinct, your first thought. While you need to be sincere and use your right intent, there is no need to over-think it as this can unnecessarily scatter your focus and dissipate energy.

**Offerings - Keywords:**

Reciprocity, Sacrifice, Giving Back

## 54   Inquire Within

## Chapter Four

## Gratitude – Being Thankful

*Everything in this world
has an equal right to live.*

Giving sincere thanks for all we have in life is one of the most powerful tools we have. Further, being grateful is a right way to live, a right way to be, whether we are consciously working with Spirit or not. I love this practice because it more easily appeals to everyone. One does not have to consider themselves to be spiritual or religious to understand or benefit from being grateful. Gratitude is easy to talk about.

Gratitude is directly related to thankfulness and appreciation. Gratitude is a positive attitude toward life which creates a positive emotion – an emotion of profound benefit to one who is experiencing it. And its feeling can grow and multiply incredibly as it is cultivated and nurtured as a way of being.

**Maintaining a grateful disposition improves virtually everything in our lives, including our health and well-being and our relationships with others.** And, importantly, being grateful displaces emotions that do not serve us – such as greed and envy – as it opens our hearts.

**The practice of gratitude involves a voluntary thankfulness for our life and all that is in it.** Gratitude is not passive. Instead, it is an active process which we consciously initiate that is not dependent on receiving anything beyond what we already have. There is an intellectual component to gratitude which is not based on emotion.

*I want what I already have.*

The practice of gratitude begins with the basics. Giving thanks for the food we eat is a productive place to start. Let us remember, dear reader, we are all kin on this planet – children of Father Sun and Mother Earth. Life continues biologically by killing life, with the guiding principle being to take only what is needed and leave the rest.

The cattle, the carrot, the corn – they all gave their lives to be on your dinner table. Giving thanks is respectful and beneficial as a way of communicating your appreciation for the life-giving sustenance you receive every single day. It helps us to understand that giving and receiving are related – like breathing in and out.

When giving thanks for my food, I like to consider all of the plants and animals which gave their lives for it. So if I'm eating breakfast, I might thank the chickens who made the eggs, thank the grain that made the bread, and thank the oranges that made the juice. I also thank the people who grew, harvested, and distributed the food. This makes me consider my place in the web of life and gives me a greater appreciation for all that I am blessed with.

In the Mayan book of creation, *Popol Vuh,* is a story which illustrates the value of gratitude from a cosmic perspective. After the Earth was formed, the Makers and Modelers decided to make human beings, and it took them four tries to do so. The first two attempts were decidedly unsuccessful. The third attempt was making humans out of wood. This worked quite well at first, but eventually problems arose. You see, the Makers and Modelers had some modest expectations about human beings – that the humans would remember who made them and be thankful to them by visiting shrines, making offerings and praying, and that they would do this in accord with the count of the sacred calendar.

Eventually the wooden people forgot who made them, forgot to give thanks, and no longer lived in harmony with the calendrical cycles of time. So the gods sent down a catastrophic rainstorm upon them. Their animals, their tools, and even their houses rose up against them with a vengeance.

The few wooden people who escaped became the monkeys in the forest.[13]

This story illustrates how Spirit's directive to remember we are divine beings is generally dismissed or forgotten by so many of us in the modern world. Cultivating gratitude is basic to living a happy, satisfying life.

There are many ways to practice gratitude. You can practice being grateful in your prayers or you can write down what you are grateful for. Some people keep a gratitude journal. Practicing gratitude will pay you back many, many times. This simple practice alone can transform your life, whether you consider yourself to be walking a spiritual path or not. This practice really helps cultivate the "why" we need in life in order to wisely choose what we do and how we do it.

Once I took a class about money and business. One presenter talked specifically about gratitude and cited it as the primary reason for his success in life. He kept coming back to the most significant factor in his success - his ongoing, continual, daily practice of gratitude. Without gratitude, his life did not have the same meaning or depth. Without gratitude, he did not realize the fullness of the gifts and blessings he had received. This gentleman had a gratitude journal, and he wrote in it every single day without fail – noting what he was grateful for.

---

[13] Translated by Dennis Tedlock, *Popul Vuh, The Definitive Edition of the Mayan Book of the Dawn of Life and the Glories of Gods and Kings* (New York, Touchstone, 1996).

*I am grateful for* _____.

**Practice not taking your life for granted, for none of us knows how many days we will be walking upon this Earth.** Our relationships with people, possessions, and circumstances are all subject to change. Viewing them through the eyes of gratitude brings out our appreciation for them and has a stabilizing influence on our life. Thanking the Divine each day for your life improves your well-being.

Here is a gratitude visualization you can try. Think of all the people in your life, those who you know and those who you do not know (who have grown your food and made your clothes at farms and factories far away, for example). Speak aloud of the gratitude you feel for them. Thank them for their presence in your life. See the faces of loved ones scrolling through your mind's eye. See the faces of friends, people you work with, teachers and others who have inspired you. Image a wave of your gratitude rolling out from you around the world, enveloping all the souls who have contributed to your life, whether or not you have ever met them. Feel the peaceful inclusion as this wave expands to ring the world in a radiant glow of thankfulness, of great gratitude for us all being here together at the same time on Earth. How wonderful it is that we are growing each other's food, building each other's shelter, and watching the same sun rise and set. Deeply thank all who share in this wonderful, glorious, planetary opportunity to experience love, healing, teaching, and learning.

Experiencing gratitude is something you can do because it is you who decides to be grateful. It is not an emotion put upon you by external forces. Being grateful for your partner, for your health, for anything important to you – even another day to live on this Earth – is like making a deposit in the cosmic bank of harmony. Feeling grateful more often will make you happier, more at ease, and more peaceful with those around you. We can find so much to be thankful for if we look at our lives honestly, gently, and without judging.

Cultivating gratitude for those closest to you in your life – your partner, your family, your co-workers, your neighbors, your friends - the people you have a responsibility for or have chosen to be with – is a powerful tonic for your well-being. So often we find it easier to be nicer to those we do not know. Yet we purposely have incarnated near to those persons who will best help us grow and expand further in this lifetime as evolving souls of Spirit.[14] Relationships are like mirrors and have much to teach us about ourselves. So let us benefit by honoring those close to us and being thankful for their presence as companions, as teachers, as awakeners.

> *Good friends*
> *more precious than gems.*

And how about giving thanks for your ancestors, and especially for those two persons whose union brought you into this world? No matter what your current relationship is with your parents – whether they are still with us on this planet or not – consider their gift as the people who facilitated your birth for the great learning and teaching you are privileged to participate in. What traits or skills did they give you which have helped you in your life? What lessons in how to be or how not to be have your parents gifted you with? Let this consideration be in gratitude, and allow the possibility of

---

[14] Michael Newton, Ph.D., *Journey of Souls, Case Studies Between Lives* (Woodbury, Llewellyn Worldwide, 1994).

the perception of your mother and father to be one of loving thankfulness.

*"Thank you, thank you, thank you."*

In 2013 Lisa and I were blessed to spend time studying and sharing in ceremony with Mayan elder Rigoberto Itzep Chanchavac in Momostenango, Guatemala. The most meaningful lesson we received was about the importance of ancestors.

The Mayan vision of the Cosmos is based on relationships – relationships between people, between people and ancestors, and between people and the Universe. The first focus is on relationships with ancestors, for everyone has ancestors – this is universal. We all have roots.

Don Rigoberto explained that there is an infinite line of generations, and we don't know how far back (or how far forward) it goes. Our parents have (or had) beliefs and customs, and maybe we don't like them. But in this chain of generations what is passed on is not the passer's fault. For example, perhaps we are gifted with creativity. We don't know how far back that attribute entered our lineage.

The first step is to recognize and accept that we have ancestors. Then we venerate them. When we don't respect our ancestors, we isolate ourselves from the line of those who came before us and are without harmony, said Don Rigoberto. When we cut ourselves off from our ancestors, we cut ourselves off from a part of our self. If we sever communications with ancestors, we are isolated and stuck. We are like a tree without our roots. Holding onto our ancestors' values is a way to retain connection with them.

When I began earnestly giving thanks for those closest to me, it coincided exactly with an improved sense of well-being in my life. It helped me look past my previous experiences of instability and chaos to a more serene and peaceful inner landscape. The practice of gratitude had a stabilizing effect on my emotions and on key relationships – such as my marriage.

> *Gratitude is not only the greatest of virtues, but the parent of all the others.*[15]
>
> ~ Cicero

Consider someone in your life, past or present, who has pushed you, challenged you, or irritated you. See how they have given you the gift of deciding for yourself what is right and what is wrong. Realize with thanks that they have helped you see who you really are, that they have given you a glimpse of your true essence. Exercises which work with our perceptions and alternative points of view can teach us a lot and help us evolve on our path.

As it is cultivated, gratitude is a feeling which builds over time and creates positive momentum in our lives. To enjoy all the things life brings us without being defined or bound by them is liberating. Ultimately we want to feel gratitude for being a spiritual being in tune with the flow of life, so that *no matter what happens, I have this!* That is the goal here – to be happy with whatever we have and no longer be dependent on possessions, friends, hobbies, or jobs to give us the value

---

[15] Marcus Tullius Cicero (Roman Philosopher and statesman ca. 106-43 BC)."

which we already inherently have in Spirit. We play our roles such as father, wife, student, or teacher without being defined by them. We are souls of pure Spirit, one with our Source, and there is nothing at all we lack.

**Gratitude - Four Tips:**

1. Voice aloud or silently each morning three things you are grateful for. Not only will gratitude become a practice, but it will begin transforming your life. When you do this, you are resonating with the energy around you and especially with the objects, situations, and people you are grateful for.

2. Silently say or think "thank you, thank you, thank you" to everyone you interact with. This will open you to the lessons of compassion and appreciation already available at every moment in every situation. We are surrounded by teachers in this world, whether or not our interaction with them feels pleasant at the time.

3. Select someone in your life who you have not liked, who you have not approved of, who irritates you, or who makes you uncomfortable. Tell yourself how grateful you are for them being in your life. Do this constantly - daily - and always when you see them or think of them. Watch how your opinion - your judgment of them and yourself - changes over time.

4. Sign an email, note, or letter "In Gratitude" when you really want to convey how much you appreciate the receiver's presence in your project or your life.

**Gratitude - Keywords:**

Appreciation, Thankfulness, Goodness

## Chapter Five

# Prayer – Speaking with Spirit

*The beauty of the world
is the beauty within.*

**The only thing we really need to know about prayer is that it works.** Everything in the Universe is made up of the same energy – plants, trees, rocks, you and me, thoughts, diseases, moons, stars; everything you can think of is made up of the same universal energy.

When we send out thoughts, wishes, dreams, or prayers, they emanate into the entire universe, and that energy has an effect. Prayer is extremely powerful. It is unbounded by space and time and unaffected by distance. You will almost certainly benefit from making prayer a part of your spiritual practice.

Prayer can be broadly defined, but it is generally a worded address to Spirit – whether spoken aloud or voiced in thought only. Prayer may be communicated through images and symbols as well. It is an act of communion, for many people including hopes or requests. When prayer focuses on a single object or theme – like peace, for instance – it comes near to the act of meditation. Prayer focusing on thankfulness is a powerful gratitude practice.

Prayer is made in so many forms. For some, it is conversation with God. For others, it is making requests. For some, it is asking for integrity or strength. And for others, it is a giving of thanks. Many people never pray for anything specific in life; they are simply drawn to a regular, daily saying of thank you in their prayers. They may ask Spirit for wisdom or clarity or courage, but don't pray for specific things to happen.

> *If the only prayer you ever say is thank you,*
> *it will be enough.*
>
> ~ Meister Eckhart [16]

My mother introduced me to a simple prayer of thanks when I was young. I forgot it for many years, and then one day it surfaced to become part of my life. It is recited after sitting down for a meal but before taking the first bite. Whether

---

[16] Meister Eckhart (German Theologian, philosopher, and mystic ca. 1260-1328).

spoken aloud or not, it feels good to do it.

> *For health and strength and daily food*
> *We give thee thanks, Oh God,*
> *Amen.*

For some people prayer takes the form of affirmations. Affirmations are declarations – a form of prayer used across the entire span of the spiritual and secular worlds. Affirmations do not rely upon the requesting style of prayer which can, at times, approach begging. There is a fine line between the two different approaches of affirming and asking. This is an important distinction to make, for we can approach prayer from the perspective that we are already whole, that what we need already exists, and that we can access what we need because we are one with it as we are one with the universe. This is a metaphysical approach to prayer.[17]

You can pray, "I am healed, I am whole," or "thank you for my healing" rather than "Please heal me, please make me whole." Do you see the difference? The idea is to connect directly with the universal Spirit which is innately within us and within all things. In fact, this is our birthright, as we were created by Spirit in Spirit's image. We do not have to cajole and beg and leverage our way into receiving that which is ours to begin with through Spirit. Let us trust in ourselves and in this great creation we are a part of and which is part

---

[17] Paramahansa Yogananda, *Journey to Self-Realization: Discovering the Gifts of the Soul* (Los Angeles, Self-Realization Fellowship, 1997).

of us. There is nothing we do not have access to through Spirit.

And if you are suffering or sick, or feeling in great need, there is a way to work with the journey from a higher perspective of peace and respect. This is honoring the cosmic process – not panicking, but being present. In this way you are working with the energetic flow of the Universe and not against it. For when you identify with Spirit, first and foremost, you are no longer identifying primarily with your body or your mood, with how the job is going, or how family life is at home. You are now traveling on a higher road – an epic journey on the path of Spirit which brings comfort to all who travel upon it.

While prayer has a great deal to do with the heartfelt path of Spirit, it also works through the powers of the mind. John Kehoe is an author and lecturer helping people move toward success and happiness by teaching about the astounding powers of their mind. Affirmation is one of the key tools he works with. Mr. Kehoe says everything in the universe is governed by laws – including people – and two of the primary laws are 1) thoughts are real forces, and 2) the mind is a sending and receiving station of thought (sending out into the universe as well as receiving the thoughts of those around us).[18] So we benefit greatly by carefully considering the content of our prayers and affirmations, as well as our state of mind and the environment around us when we make them.

**Words have power!**

---

[18] John Kehoe, *Mind Powers Into the 21st Century, Techniques to Harness the Astounding Powers of Thought* (Vancouver, Zoetic Inc., 1997).

When you state your affirmation, you are declaring a personal truth to yourself which also travels from you in every direction and dimension. Any thought you have or statement you make travels this same way. Transmitting like a radio signal, your affirmation resonates throughout the Universe and eventually echoes back to you to grow in your life. Prayer, therefore, is like planting a seed.

Whether the truth affirmed is something already true for you in your life or something you want to be true, it is made real in the realm of possibility and manifestation by the powerful act of speaking it confidently, regularly, and with humble conviction. Affirmations can be the blueprinting of what will be. In Christian mythology, "First there was the Word." For the Hindus, the sound *Aum* (or *Om*) created the universe. Matter originating from sound is an ancient idea and a cosmology that still rings true today.

> *One oral utterance, which boldly states how you want your life to be, is worth more than dozens of books read or lectures attended.*
>
> ~ Catherine Ponder[19]

When you approach prayer as affirmation – of declaring personal truth – you are engaging all the energy of the universe to support and sustain you; you are not reaching for something you do not have or for something not yours. Rather, you are affirming the inherent spiritual nature of your

---

[19] Catherine Ponder, *Open Your Mind to Receive* (Marina del Rey, DeVorss & Company, 1983.

existence as a soul of Spirit currently residing in your great body temple.

Affirmation, by its nature, is widely applicable and ranges from the secular and grounded to the spiritual and high-flying. Writing down affirmations and then reciting them magnifies their effectiveness. Using the present tense moves the affirmative prayer from a future wish into a present possibility. It is like sending out a broadcast to the Universe. Here are some sample affirmations:

> *I do what needs to be done when it needs to be done.*
> *I live within my means.*
> *I am kind to everyone, and everyone is kind to me.*
> *I am in harmony with all things.*
> *I am a divine soul of pure Spirit.*
> *I honor my body temple.*
> *I am healthy, I am whole.*
> *I and Spirit are one.*
> *Through Spirit I have everything.*
> *I trust in the process of life.*
> *All that I need is always taken care of.*
> *I am safe.*

Prayer, according to Michael Bernard Beckwith, Founder and Spiritual Director of Agape International Spiritual Center, is the most powerful technology we have today.[20] Prayer can be even more powerful after meditation, as a quieting of the mind puts us into a calmer, clearer space. Even just taking a few deep breaths before praying can help. Then we are led more by the heart than the mind and come into harmony with

---

[20] Michael Bernard Beckwith, www.agapelive.com.

our self. In this state of clarity, we are better able to consider the merits of what we wish to pray for and make the prayer most appropriate for us.

Whatever you pray for, Spirit workers from all walks of life counsel to leave the means to the desired end in God's hands. Spirit works in mysterious ways, and we do not want to limit its power by being too specific, or we cut ourselves off from the unlimited, infinite creativity of the Universe. It is helpful to remember the well-known words, "Not my will, but thy will." Spirit's plans are not always visible, and it is not always about what we want but rather about what we need (sometimes called the Will of God or the Will of Heaven). "May thy will be done" is a nice way to finish a prayer.

"Always make sure that everything is as it should be," counsels spiritual teacher, Mary Magdalene of the Cross.[21] At first these words were supremely challenging because sometimes I did not feel things were as they should be. Maybe I was unhappy or feeling stressed or worried. "How could everything possibly be as it should be?" I thought to myself. "It sure doesn't seem like it!" But as I practiced and used the power of the affirmation, "Everything is as it should be" to influence how I chose to perceive life, I found it increasingly easier to accept my life and find a harmonious way forward.

On days when I'll be attending an important meeting or function, I say a prayer beforehand that goes like this.

> *Oh Great Spirit -*
> *In my interactions and meetings with others*

---

[21] Mary Magdalene of the Cross (Temple of the Deer Wisdom School).

> *on this fine day*
> *may I be blessed to listen more than I speak.*
> *May I carry myself with humility,*
> *with honor, and with non-judgement,*
> *and may the product of our interactions*
> *be for the greater good of all.*
> *May the blessings be,*
> *Aum, Peace, Amen.*

Prayers are best to always be *for* something rather than against something. Negative energies propagate throughout the Universe in accord with the same laws that deliver positive energies. Additionally, the Universe does not seem to recognize words such as "no," "not," or "don't." Thus we benefit by stating "I am healthy," for example, rather than saying "I am not sick," which can actually work against us.[22] Again, it is worthwhile to carefully consider the content of our prayers and make them in a space where we are calm and unhurried.

If you are ever wondering about what to pray for, you might consider including in your practice a daily prayer or visualization for a better world. The Mayan elders in Guatemala advise that it is beneficial if we take some time each day to imagine a better world.[23] We can imagine a better world for our family and our friends; for our children and our children's children; for all whom we know and all whom we do not know; for the animals and plants of this great planet that sustain us. It is good to do this at the end of the day, the

---

[22] Drew Heriot and Sean Byrne, *The Secret* (Prime Time Productions, 2006).

[23] Carlos Barrios, The Prophets Conference

elders tell us, and to light a candle as well, so the light may work to overcome the darkness and ignorance in our world.

When I was a little boy, the Peace Prayer of St. Francis was framed on the wall by my bedside – a gift from my maternal grandmother. The prayer occurs in many variations and is attributed to St. Francis of Assisi in the 13th century. While it cannot be traced back that far in history, it is nevertheless a beautiful and effective expression of peace.

> *Lord, make me an instrument of your peace;*
> *where there is hatred, let me sow love;*
> *when there is injury, pardon;*
> *where there is doubt, faith;*
> *where there is despair, hope;*
> *where there is darkness, light;*
> *and where there is sadness, joy.*
> *Grant that I may not so much seek*
> *to be consoled as to console;*
> *to be understood, as to understand,*
> *to be loved as to love;*
> *for it is in giving that we receive,*
> *it is in pardoning that we are pardoned,*
> *and it is in dying (to ourselves) that we are born*
> *to eternal life.*

Prayer is often reserved only for emergencies when no other "normal" means of assistance seem to have worked. This indicates how materialistic our culture is, since prayer and communicating with Spirit are not commonly included in our society's tool bag for the everyday challenges and blessings in life.

Contemporary spiritual teacher Ram Dass speaks of a useful prayer when one is unsure or scared, and it has value as a regular prayer to remind us of our relationship with Spirit: "The power of God is within me. The grace of God surrounds me."[24] This is a prayer of protection which can be repeated over and over.

Ongoing communication with Spirit in this way gently and lovingly works the garden of your soul so you may heal and grow. Prayer puts you in a place where you are swimming in the natural abundance of the universe – where you are in the flow of it all. Once there you can make the right prayers in the right way so they interact with the Cosmos in a harmonious and effective manner.

The following prayer from the Navajo tradition directly addresses this style of prayer – acknowledging the beauty of Mother Earth, the Universe and, by extension, the beauty of the one who speaks it.

> *With beauty before me, I walk*
> *With beauty behind me, I walk*
> *With beauty above me, I walk*
> *With beauty below me, I walk*
> *From the East beauty has been renewed*
> *From the South beauty has been renewed*
> *From the West beauty has been renewed*
> *From the North beauty has been renewed*
> *From the zenith in the sky beauty has been renewed*
> *From the nadir of the Earth beauty has been renewed*

---

[24] Ram Dass with Stephen Levine, *Grist for the Mill* (New York, Bantam Books, 1977).

*From all around me beauty has been renewed*[25]

Marking the location of our life within sacred space is a majestic and moving practice. Acknowledging the participation of the directions in our lives places us within them, where we are guided and protected by their embracing and sustaining powers. All our ancestral traditions draw deeply from directional wisdom.

There can also be great power in praying with others. Many traditions do this, and it is a fact that a prayer's power increases when conducted by a group – regardless of whether the persons involved are together in one location or dispersed around the world. Remember, prayer is unaffected by distance.

People all around the planet pray each day for peace. Because the sun is always shining on half the globe, peace prayers are ongoing, 24 hours a day. These prayers may have held our world together more than we know during this era where ignorance and violence can be so prevalent.

Prayer, as we have seen, is one of the ways we regain and maintain the awareness of our innate wholeness as divine creatures of the Cosmos. In the last chapter we learned a bit from the Mayan creation story *Popol Vuh*, when the Makers and Modelers attempted for the third time to make human beings. They made a fourth, and last, attempt.

This fourth time, a fox, a coyote, a parrot, and a crow tell the Makers and Modelers about yellow corn and white corn

---

[25] This anonymous Navajo prayer, in many versions, has appeared abundantly in books and on Web sites.

growing on a mountain, and they use it to make humans. These new human beings remember their makers and pray to them. And not only that, they also have vision and knowledge as perfect as the gods! This alarmed the Makers and Modelers, and so they decided to put a fog upon their eyes, so human beings would not so easily "see" their true divine nature.[26]

We are removing the fog from our eyes. We are parting the mystical veil between worlds to realize the divine nature of all things. This veil was not put there by us. We are not to fault ourselves for what we feel has been missing from our lives. We can combine proven spiritual techniques with awareness and self-responsibility to awaken into our destiny as cosmic beings living peacefully in community on Planet Earth.

In closing the subject of prayer, it is worthwhile examining two words which are often used to conclude prayers – *Aum* and *Amen*. These words are ubiquitous in the individual cultures which employ them.

*Aum* (or *Om*) symbolizes the Supreme Divine in its feminine creative aspect of the universe. Said to be the foundation of Hindu prayer, it is an ancient, sacred Sanskrit syllable uttered as a *mantra* and believed to be the original, primordial sound of the universe. *Mantras*, which will be discussed in the next chapter, are simple sounds or series of words which have transformative qualities. Hindu *mantras* usually begin and end with *Aum*.

---

[26] Translated by Dennis Tedlock, *Popul Vuh, The Definitive Edition of the Mayan Book of the Dawn of Life and the Glories of Gods and Kings* (New York, Touchstone, 1996).

*Amen*, of Hebrew origin, is traditionally uttered as the conclusion of a prayer as way of approval, to intensify its effects and honor its power. It is variously translated to mean truly, verily, so be it, and let it be. Commonly used within Christianity, Judaism, and Islam, *Amen* is also used in a secular manner as a word to confer strong agreement. While not academically supported, it has been said that *Aum* and *Amen* (as well as the Egyptian *Amun*) share a common root.

Offerings, gratitude, and prayer seem to be versions of each other – overlapping, interweaving, and empowering each other. As a dynamic triad they work together to create a soulful depth and a noticeable momentum in our lives. Indeed, May the Blessings Be.

**Prayer - Three Tips:**

1. Be absolutely clear about what you are praying for and what your motives are. Be careful what you wish for or, as the Talking Heads lyric goes, "Watch out, you might get what you're after."

2. Take a moment before praying or affirming to let your body and mind slow down and relax. This allows you to resonate more harmonically with the energy of the Universe.

3. Select three positive declarations about your life and voice them as affirmations each day. Do this for 30 days straight upon rising, in the middle of the day, and again before bed. This will help you realize the benefit and bring the practice of prayer into your life as a habit.

**Prayer - Keywords:**

Affirmation, Declaration, Petition, Request

78    Inquire Within

## Chapter Six

# Meditation – Communing with Spirit

*May we be blessed
to stop moving
stop doing
stop thinking
stop everything
and behold the splendor
and gentle grace.*

There is something wonderful about sitting quietly with no requirement to do a single thing at all. Allowing the breath to reach its natural rhythm and not forcing anything, we may notice far off sounds which come into the room. Allowing the mind to do what it wants - just watching it as an observer -

we see the thoughts that arise, and then let them drift and float away.

We become detached from these thoughts, for they are like a passing show. They are not the essence of who we are. The longer we sit, the quieter we get, the more still we are, and the more we relax. We begin noticing the still center around which this world of whirling thoughts exists. Being present in the here and now is the beginning of meditation. It is the process of becoming not just aware, but awareness itself.

Meditation is defined in many ways. It is a self-directed practice for relaxing the body and calming the mind. It is self-regulation of attention in the process of self-discovery. It is a mental discipline through which one attempts to go beyond the thinking mind into a deeper state of awareness. Still another definition is concentration on God - interiorizing attention and focusing on some aspect of God.

In his beautiful book on meditation entitled *A Gradual Awakening*, Stephen Levine boils it down for us when he writes, *"Meditation is awareness."*[27] Central to Buddhism and many other traditions, meditation is considered a vital tool in spiritual development. Yet it is practiced both within and outside religious tradition because of its many proven benefits.

**Meditation is about cultivating the mind and developing awareness.** Awareness overpowers and neutralizes the controlling ego (our thoughts and concepts) to let us glimpse the ever-present observer (the consciousness behind them).

---

[27] Stephen Levine, *A Gradual Awakening* (New York, Anchor Books, 1979).

Awareness reveals our true being which is timeless and joyful.

Meditation has the capacity to reset us to our natural state of balance and harmony with the Universe. Consciousness researcher Itzhak Bentov noted that, when we are in the meditative state, the electrostatic field of our bodies goes into resonance with the electric field of the Earth.[28] According to Mr. Bentov, a deeply meditating human being and the Earth come into resonance with each other, transferring energy back and forth. This is a momentous fact which calls for our contemplation as we become more serious about our personal evolution and our place in the web of life. This research indicates our innate ability to be in harmony with the Earth, and even the Sun, the Milky Way, and deep space (as wider fields of resonance we can enter into).

As we sit in stillness, we are able to see thoughts about our life rise up and float away like bubbles in the air. The awareness developed through meditation shows us that our mistakes, our bad habits, and our negative emotions are not who we really are. They depend entirely on our thoughts and our state of mind to exist. And so we can begin learning not to identify with our thoughts and, as a result, not to experience the suffering that is associated with some of them, especially negative, disempowering thoughts.

Just as there are many definitions of meditation, there are also many meditation techniques. A common method is where the meditator sits quietly, centering awareness on a process such as the breath, a *mantra*, or a visualization. This technique is called single-pointed meditation. Its goal is to stabilize the

---

[28] Itzhak Bentov, *Stalking the Wild Pendulum, On the Mechanics of Consciousness* (New York, Bantam Books, 1977).

mind by reining it, in so it can be under our control. Thoughts are not viewed as intrusions. Instead, they are just noticed without attachment in the process of remaining present. A variation on this method involves total concentration on a single object or process and, when the mind strays, it is purposefully drawn back to the chosen object or process.

In analytical meditation one concentrates on a particular subject such as kindness, impermanence, or emptiness. We meditate point by point on all facets of the subject. Turning it over in our mind, looking at all angles and all the pros and cons, we study it deeply.

I treasure meditation time. Just sitting without any burden, without need to do anything else, I can be without pretense. One reason I believe my meditation has deepened is due to the room I have created to practice in. I consider it a temple, a place that causes me to be peaceful and calm and which turns me toward Spirit. It adds spice to the recipe for spiritual sustenance.

Carry a small candle with you on your travels. If you are in a hotel room or in the guest bedroom of a friend's house, you can pull out the little candle, light it, and have a short meditation or make a prayer. It is like carrying your own portable sacred space with you. Doing this will set the tone for your day and allow you to cultivate spaciousness and equanimity no matter where you are.

You can meditate whenever and wherever it feels good for you to do so. It can be in your own special space inside or in the cool shade under a tree in the backyard or on the beach where the sound of the waves caresses and cleanses your mind and body. Don't get psyched out by the notion that meditation has to produce deep insights and big spiritual fireworks to qualify as a success. Just being, relaxing, releasing tension and letting go is a good start and worthwhile in itself.

Meditation

Early morning is a perfect time to meditate. After you arise from sleep the mind is quiet and well suited to remaining that way a bit longer. If you want to concentrate your mind, it is rested and easier to direct. Late evening is also a good time to meditate, just before bed. This allows your energies, which may have been scattered by the restless activities of the day, to become peaceful again.

**To meditate, sit however it is comfortable for you.** You can sit in a cross-legged position on a thick pillow on the floor. This way your back is straight and you do not have to work to remain in an upright position. You can kneel, you can sit in a chair, or you can even lie on your back. Find a position that feels comfortable – one that you can maintain while keeping your back straight. This allows for smooth flow of energy. In many traditions the meditator sits in a cross-legged form which allows the body to take the general shape of a pyramid. One position, with your bottom and two knees touching the ground, is very stable and aids in your ability to remain still and in the same position for a long time. This, in turn, allows you to tune in more with your body's energetic field (also called the luminous energy field or light body).

There are some sophisticated meditation methods involving specific exercises with the breath. Get started by taking a few deep breaths through your nose, letting each one out slowly through your mouth - sighing if you need to - releasing tension as you exhale. It is fine if your release is loud; it just means you are letting go of tension and stress. This preparation relaxes and settles you. After a moment, you will feel calmer and be able to sit more easily. Breathe in and out through your nose while meditating. This is more effective than mouth breathing, as it gives you more tranquility and more energy at the same time, as more oxygen is circulated through your brain and body. Rest your tongue gently behind your teeth, on the roof of your mouth, to prevent saliva build-up.

You may find it uncomfortable to sit for very long when you first start meditating. At first, even five minutes of being still can be a challenge and seem interminably long. And, of course, the mind doesn't want to stop thinking and will go on chattering about anything and everything until it tires or until your object of focus eclipses it. Meditation trainer and Shaktipat Master Steven Sadleir says you can allow your mind to run on with its thoughts, like a television left on in the other room. You don't need to pay attention to it or worry about it. Just leave it running in the background.[29]

Be patient and gentle with yourself. Tell yourself there is nothing that needs to be done. Give yourself permission to relax. Try to sit for longer periods of time as you get into your practice. Before long you may find twenty minutes has gone by just like that, for the deep space meditation takes us into is outside time.

It can help to go through a relaxation checklist to calm and quiet and relax the body. Once you have sat down and relaxed by taking some deep breaths, imagine someone slowly and peacefully saying:

> *Relax your feet*
> *Relax your knees*
> *Relax your legs*
> *Relax your pelvis*
> *Relax your gut*
> *Relax your chest*
> *Relax your hands*
> *Relax your arms*
> *Relax your shoulders*
> *Relax your neck*
> *Relax your jaw*
> *Relax your eyes*

---

[29] Steven S. Sadleir (Self Awareness Institute, http://selfawarenessnow.com).

*Relax your forehead*

Take your time going through this checklist and you will become aware of the different parts of your body and how much tension you are holding in them. You will notice that awareness of your body actually causes it to relax. In this process you see how you are holding stress and rigidity and are able to begin letting it go, so that it may dissipate. Relaxing your jaw and shoulders, in particular, can make an immediate difference in how you feel. Body awareness is critical.

Observe your body and the life force informing it, circulating through it, and powering it. Notice the curious, interesting, placid nature of the space you are in. This "observer mode" awareness is the foundation of meditation. The more you sit in meditation, the more you will notice a space of peace begins to open. Eventually you will find this space has always been there inside you, a timeless part of yourself - your original essence.

You can visualize the mechanical process of meditation by imagining your busy thinking mind as a mud puddle. When you first sit down to meditate, the puddle is muddy and you cannot see through the silt to the bottom. As time goes by, the suspended particles (your thoughts) slowly settle to the bottom and the water (your mind) becomes clear. At this point you began to see the essence of yourself – the magnificent and uniquely interesting geography at the bottom of the puddle. Sitting in still silence helps us realize our true nature. Disengaging from thoughts and emotions, we can be truly present in the simple joy and contentment of being.

As you stop identifying with your thoughts, the world takes on a presence where everything simply is. This "is-ness" mirrors the calm, quiet, unjudging center within you. When you make room to be in the time that is outside time you are healed and refreshed. This is, in fact, your natural state – a state of peace. Your identity – what you identify with – is only a small part of who you are.

When the mind is quiet it can be directed in any way we wish. We come to know this with repeated practice. Our thinking mind endeavors to be our master, yet we need the wisdom of our body and our intuition as well. There is liberation and freedom to be found in meditation, and it is beyond our body and even beyond our mind. Our minds are incredibly small when compared to the great universal ocean of consciousness which is Spirit itself. Yet we can expand our being to encompass more and more of Spirit and reflect more and more of Spirit in our lives.

**Meditation brings us back to that part of us which resides always in the realm of Spirit, which connects us to all that is.** Meditation in its highest forms brings us to God. This is why meditation is so important in so many spiritual traditions. It is communion with Spirit in our inner temple.

Our inner temple is the perfect place to ask the great questions of existence: Who am I? Where did I come from? Why am I here? What is the meaning of life? Eventually these questions are answered within our place of inner knowing, where the self and Spirit are one. Ours is a journey to return to our source, a return to the awareness of our union with Spirit, to sail from the wide-ranging rivers of many into the inevitable ocean of oneness.

There are other forms of meditation, loosely categorized as energy practices or movement meditation, which can provide immense benefit. These practices are ancient paths of harmony and healing involving visualization and physical movement. They integrate body, mind, soul, and Spirit, and can significantly affect positive health. Movement meditation stills the mind and puts the body back into resonance and accord with universal energy.

*Yoga, Qigong, Tai Chi,* and chanting are some of the most popular movement meditations and a good place to start. If it is difficult for you to sit still in meditation, one of these disciplines may work well for you. These practices serve to ground and root you, calm you, and quiet your mind, and yet they energize you in an incredibly positive way.[30]

One of the virtues of movement is that we have to concentrate on our body, and this causes our thinking mind to take a back seat to the physical process at hand. Our mind is engaged on the movement rather than its usual parade of thoughts. Much energy is generated and cycled through the body during movement and, while this takes energy to accomplish, we are ultimately charged and rejuvenated within a nonverbal state – just as we are with formal meditation.

*Yoga* comes from a Sanskrit word meaning yoke or union. Most commonly *yoga* is thought of as the physical positions called *asanas,* which are used to relax, tone, and align the body. However this discipline also uses breathing techniques and meditation to quiet and clarify the mind. *Yoga* methods are designed to help one achieve enlightenment or cosmic

---

[30] There is a difference between grounding and rooting. Grounding is a centering and balancing. Rooting is deeper; it is an anchoring into the Earth itself, like a tree root.

consciousness – the direct experience of communion with Spirit.

*Qigong* (pronounced "chee-gung") is an ancient Chinese healing art and medicine combining meditation, movement, and regulation of breathing which benefits all aspects of health. It cultivates the accumulation of *Chi* energy, or life force. The flowing movements of *Qigong* are generally gentler than the still postures of *Yoga*. As such, it is very suitable for a diverse range of ages, body types, and physical conditions.

Practicing Tai Chi

*Tai Chi* is another Chinese system of healing movement. It is both a martial art and a form of *Qigong*. Most people practice it solely as a complex Qigong for its many wellness benefits. It combines meditation with slow, gentle physical exercises which cause relaxation and develop balance and health. Appearing almost as a dance, *Tai Chi* is a graceful, energizing practice that can be deeply satisfying. Practicing *Qigong* and *Tai Chi* regularly has benefitted my health, made me more relaxed, and given me a practice which complements and supports my daily meditation.

Chanting is basically singing in a rhythmic, repetitive tone. In India and elsewhere, people chant *mantras* which are simple sounds or a series of words which have transformative qualities. *Mantras* are vibrations of raw sound that resonate deeply with those who sing them and also positively affect the environment around them. Perhaps the simplest, and some say the most powerful, *mantra* is chanting *Aum,* also written as *Om*. *Aum* is revered as the primordial sound of the Universe, and it is said the chanting of *Aum* alone will transform the one who sings it.

The sounds of *mantras* are powerful vibrations which activate matter. They are like seeds planted in our conscious mind. Through repetition and acceptance they sink their roots deeply into our unconscious mind, where the power of the *mantra* is activated.

In experiments subjecting sound to fine sand distributed on top of a thin sheet of metal, the simple vowel components of *mantras* were found to create specific shapes out of the sand. When the vowel "O" was sounded, the sand took the round shape of "O" on the metal plate.

Different vowels vibrate different parts of the body. "Ah," for example, vibrates the upper chest and heart area, while "Oo" resonates the lower abdominal area. Not only does sound affect our mindsets and moods, but also our endocrine glands, internal organs, and our cellular fluid balance. This subject, including detailed information about *mantras*, is discussed at length in Randall McClellan's in-depth book, *The Healing Forces of Music*.[31] Serious *mantra* work needs to be done under the guidance of a teacher. There can be danger in chanting without really knowing what effect it will have.

If you are drawn to more active, energetic chanting, you can probably find a chapter of the Nichiren Buddhists of Soka Gakkai International in your area. The members of S.G.I. chant in prayer and are providing value to people all around the world who want to practice spirituality within a community that understands the quickening pace of the times we live in.

Other, perhaps less obvious, forms of movement meditation include walking, running, hiking, swimming, and playing music. In meditative walking, one foot is placed in front of the other, slowly, gently, purposefully, and you are totally absorbed in it – living fully in the present moment. These types of activities take you into a zone, an altered state of consciousness. Anything can be done as a meditation if you are not thinking as much as you are focusing on the process, becoming one with it.

**Your entire life can be lived as a meditation.**

Meditation has proven health benefits for both mind and body. Reducing anxiety, lowering blood pressure, and helping to manage chronic pain are all documented results of

---

[31] Randall McClellan, Ph.D., *The Healing Forces of Music, History, Theory and Practice* (Warwick, Amity House, 1988).

meditation. It is an ancient practice that is becoming more popular, seemingly in correlation with our need to live more peaceful and less stressful lives.

Meditation is also a mirror for seeing what is happening in our lives from a nonjudgmental perspective. In observer mode we can easily see what we are stuck on, pondering, or hoping for. When we notice these things, we are able to see our lives from a higher, more compassionate perspective.

One of the great benefits of meditation is that it teaches us patience. Take waiting, for example – waiting in line, waiting for an appointment, waiting at a traffic light. Waiting is an opportunity to observe the present moment with undivided attention, noticing the colors, the smells, the sounds, and the movement. We see our world anew, *as it is,* unfolding, rather than experience frustration or inconvenience by our delay in waiting. The virtue of patience is delighting in the fascination and even amusement available in the ever-present moment.

> *There is nowhere to go & there is nothing to do.*
>
> *~ Ram Dass*[32]

**Meditation helps us build strength by teaching us to be less reliant on material things, less affected by emotions, and less dependent on the state of our bodies as a measure of how we feel about life.** Meditation brings us back into the eternal now and helps us realize our own intuitive wisdom and insight.

---

[32] Ram Dass, *Be Here Now* (Lama Foundation, 1971).

As you meditate more, you may be amazed at what comes to you intuitively. There could be a solution to a particular problem or insight about an issue from a perspective you had never considered before. You may envision some action which had never before entered your mind. The more you meditate, the more you and universal mind are connecting.

In the present exist the answers to all questions and the secret to all things. Illumination is not found in the past, looking backwards, or in the future, looking forward. Being present, *now* – this is where fulfillment and meaning reside, rich with the goodness of life.

Spiritual teacher Eckhart Tolle writes beautifully of how waiting for the future to give us those things we want in life is actually a rejection of the present.[33] When we are so focused on a future where we will feel better about our life, we experience a lack of quality in our present. Meditation – the practice of being aware (in whatever we are doing) – gives us back the very wholeness we are striving for. With practice and commitment we can relearn to live with the same fascination about the world we had as children.

You can research different meditation techniques to discover what works best for you. Take a meditation class, listen to a guided meditation CD, or learn about it in a book. With the guidance of a teacher you may more easily receive the instruction and grasp the essence of the method. In-person instruction also allows you to feed off the teacher's direction and inspiration.

---

[33] Eckhart Tolle, *The Power of Now, A Guide to Spiritual Enlightenment* (Vancouver, Namaste Publishing, 2004).

**Meditation – Three Tips:**

1. It is more effective to meditate ten minutes each day than it is to meditate once a week for an hour. Take small, sure steps and know they are worthwhile steps. This is not a competition or a race.

2. Be patient and do not expect quick results. Benefit comes whether or not you notice it at first, so do not be dissuaded. If you enjoy sitting at all in meditation, then you are already receiving benefit.

3. Stare at a candle, observe and follow the rhythm of your breath, hold a stone in your hand, or listen to the sounds around you as a technique to focus single-pointedly on an object or a process. This can help you move beyond the habitual focus on thoughts and jumpstart your meditation practice.

**Meditation – Keywords:**

Awareness, Mindfulness, Being

# Chapter Seven

# Solitude – Being With Nature

*The Great Solitude opens my heart.*

One of the best ways to become more in touch with your spirituality and to develop a sense of your kinship with all things is by spending time in Nature. Often, even if we know it is good for us to be outdoors, we get too busy and we have too many obligations or excuses (it's too far away; I don't have enough time). We unwittingly deny ourselves the irreplaceable experience of our basic, fundamental, life-affirming connection with the Earth.

Nature is defined broadly as the natural world, the material world, and the physical universe we live in. Nature is often more specifically defined as Earth's wilderness – the natural environment which has not been altered significantly by human activity.

Humankind, however, is part of the natural world and cannot escape being so. The western philosophy of Man versus Nature has effectively obscured this fact from our awareness and removed it from our predominant value system. This is a significant factor in how out of balance humanity is with the rest of Nature at this time in history. Our race grew out of the Earth just like the trees, but we seem to have collective amnesia about this vital fact. A critical difference between a man and a tree is that man has a choice to act in harmony with Nature or to be in dissonance against it. This is the dynamic of Man as Nature versus Man against Nature.

> *Man does not weave this web of life. He is merely a strand of it. Whatever he does to the web, he does to himself.*
>
> *~ Chief Seattle*[34]

There is an underlying assumption in our modern culture that we human beings are kings of Nature. In this paradigm we assume we are in charge of it, and it is here for us to use as we wish – as witnessed by unchecked resource exploitation at the expense of widespread animal and plant life, as well as of human health. This mindset obliterates our awareness of the inescapable reality of our deep connection with all things in the web of life. It causes us to live life out of balance, and it bypasses the noble idea that we can become

---

[34] Chief Seattle (Duwamish leader ca. 1780-1866).

caretakers or stewards of the Earth, serving on behalf of all life that lives here.

My intention is not to debate the morals and ethics around this critical point. Rather, it is to consider that being with Nature allows us to come back into harmony with it and, accordingly, back into harmony with ourselves. It is about *being Nature*.

When walking in the forest, I am enchanted by the trees and feel a kinship with them not unlike the kinship I feel with fellow human beings. I may come across a particularly wonderful tree and say, "Hello, old friend, it is so good to see you. Look at you, look at you! You are beautiful!" Talking to the trees, talking to the birds and the natural world around us, deeply enhances our experience of connection with our world.

Some may think it strange to talk with a tree, but let me assure you it is a reasonable and a productive thing to do. Our indigenous ancestors all communicated with the natural world and heard echoes back from it in the form of insights, knowledge, and wisdom. Our ancestors knew they were part of Nature and that Nature was part of them. It was not strange to them if a plant advised them how to heal their sick brother or sister.

Here is a simple way you can talk with Nature. Go for a walk in a park or just stroll down the street where you live. As you move along on your way, greet the world around you. "Hello, trees; hello, bushes; hello, ferns; hello, sky; hello, clouds; hello, birds," and so on, acknowledging all that are there. "Hello, dragonflies; hello, stones; hello, houses." It can be a wonderful thing.

Mt Baker-Snoqualmie National Forest

Communicating with Nature helps wake up the part of us that is aware deep inside, that knows in our bones we are part of the same community – that we are one. At a deep level we know we are living in a world of interconnection and interdependency.

So don't be shy. Don't think to yourself "What am I doing? I must be off my rocker; I'm talking to a tree!" Allow yourself to try this and work with it over time. With grace you will feel the medicine of this path. You will see it in the way you feel about yourself and the world around you. It will bring forth that playful, innocent part of you that may have been hiding quietly within since childhood.

The feeling of harmony and joy received from being outdoors comes home with us and affects our lives in a wonderfully healthy way. Repeated visits in Nature increase this benefit over time and improve the way we feel in our home life, in our social life, and even in our work life.

When we say we need to "get some air," it is often more than that. Being outside makes us feel better. We have an unconscious need to be with the sky and the Earth because we are part of it. This is the world which relaxes and energizes us and gives us all we need to live. Outdoors, our luminous energy field, or aura – which extends beyond the skin of our body – is less compressed by walls or ceilings and less affected by mental stresses as well. Our luminous energy field is akin to our essence, our original, true being that resides always in Spirit. As such, this is profound medicine – tree medicine, rock medicine, sky medicine, water medicine. Almost magically it clears our minds and opens our hearts. Being in Nature reawakens within us the joy of experiencing raw, unfiltered beauty. With grace we may discover this same beauty exists also within us at the core of our being.

> *To be in a place*
> *of grace and precious beauty*
> *teaches me to see.*

Perhaps you are attracted to the mountains or to the forest. Maybe it's the ocean, a certain lake, or a river which makes you feel a sense of peace and well-being every time you are there. Maybe it's the desert or a park in the city where you live. Your spirit, your soul, your mind, your body - they know when they are feeling good. So listen to them and go to the places which create this feeling for you. If this is a new concept for you, just choose a place outdoors, go there, and see what happens.

Being alone in Nature, we are not in conversation with other people. Our thought processes are able to naturally slow down and, with patience and grace, to dwindle significantly from how they fill our minds in day-to-day life. It is a form of meditation in which the environment is the object of our focus. A larger space within us begins to open and peacefulness blesses us deeply with its presence. We are subsequently more open to insights and self-realization. What we want to change and what we want to affirm in our lives becomes more easily self-evident.

**The clarity gained by being alone with Nature opens us to receiving intuitive information and epiphanies.**

> *The world is all Love.*
> *It's here,*
> *Without asking to be*
> *Recognized,*
> *Taken care of,*
> *Classified,*
> *Divided or polluted.*
> *It simply is as it is,*
> *With no ulterior motives.*
> *The world is unconditional –*
> *And that which is unconditional*
> *is Love.*

I learned a lesson about truth from a mountain lake when I circumnavigated its perimeter on a glorious fall day. Its shape changed, and its color varied as I moved along the shore, and I realized each of us sees life from our own individual point of view. Each perspective from around the circle of life is equally valid. This Nature teaching helped me better appreciate that each of our life paths are different, yet they are of equal value and ultimately lead to the same place. It helped me learn we can accept and respect each other, and we do not need to quarrel over which view is right.

Contemplation at Evolution Lake

Let us consider for a moment the practical value we derive from Mother Earth. She provides us with the air we breathe, the food we eat, and the fresh water we drink. She gives us shade from the sun and the plentiful healing plant medicines. How we value Nature and how we feel about Nature are ultimately crucial to our personal experience of dwelling on this planet within the web of life that sustains us. A sense of caring for the Earth and the Cosmos which nurture us deepens the value we feel.

We have a choice whether we want to engage in the responsibilities of being a caretaker of the Earth. When we say "yes" to this choice, it positively impacts our practice of gratitude. For we are then participating consciously in the web of life, realizing kindness as a virtue, and connecting with ancient wisdom which has, at its core, a base of deep reverence for the Earth.

These words are not written to inflict guilt or to place unwanted responsibility on your shoulders. I am simply inviting you to participate more deeply in the fullness of this grand existence you are part of, as a planetary citizen in community with all who share this world.

As noted earlier, giving an offering to Mother Earth is a powerful act of reciprocity. She bears us, clothes us, feeds us, shelters us, and in the end She receives our bodies unconditionally. This is most certainly a definition of love. Giving Her something of value as an offering or payment for being taken care of is a practical thing to do.

> *All are but parts of one stupendous whole,*
> *whose body is nature and God the Soul.*
>
> *~ Alexander Pope*[35]

---

[35] Alexander Pope (English Poet, 1688-1744).

Communion

Dedication and repetition work in virtually all human endeavors, and they will do so here. Go outdoors, allow yourself time so you are not hurried, and see what happens. Camping is a great way to experience Nature. It is astounding what insights and illumination begin to occur after a few days in the wilderness. I cannot overemphasize the value of being outdoors.

Nature gives to us our power animals and allies, the elements, and many of the archetypes which for millennia have supported and inspired us. We may find an affinity for an animal like Eagle and realize it is teaching us about being in the world. We relate to Eagle, and it comes to represent an aspect of our existence. We derive power from this, and it becomes a power animal for us. For others, it may be Wolf, Ant, Whale, or Tree which speaks to them. There are myriad ways Nature communicates. Nature is where our spiritual and our physical existence meet and play out. Nature can truly nourish our soul on its epic journey of transformation.

This brings us to a particular technique called the Vision Quest.

> *A very great vision is needed*
> *and the man who has it must follow it*
> *as the Eagle seeks the deepest blue of the sky.*
>
> ~ *Chief Crazy Horse*[36]

**The vision quest is an ancient spiritual and life practice.** It involves going alone into the wilderness and remaining there until a vision appears. In Native American traditions, a person – usually a young person – would be escorted to a particular place in Nature and then left there, instructed not to return to his or her village until a vision was received. The

---

[36] Chief Crazy Horse (Oglala Lakota leader ca. 1840-1877).

# Solitude – Being with Nature

vision received might profoundly influence one's path in life or, in some cases, even the path of the tribe.

In the hustle and bustle of so-called civilized life, there is rarely the time and space available which allow visions and intuitions to reveal themselves. The pace is so fast we don't create room for them. Therefore it is up to us to make the effort – to meet Spirit halfway. This effort is always rewarded.

Even if you only have a few hours, that is still an opportunity to go outdoors, to be silent and still and ask for a vision, clarity on a life issue, or a higher overview of one's life. When you make yourself a proper vessel – by going to a suitable place with a receptive attitude – you will, with grace, receive what you are looking for. Or perhaps, you will receive what you need at this moment in your life.

Mt. Rainier National Park

*The Grove*

*So high*
*so huge*
*so handsome*
*to visit you is an honor*
*to touch you is ten-fold*
*the birdsong begins*
*to tell of your beauty*
*but it would have to sing*
*for a thousand years.*


Take a small daypack with you on your Nature outings so you can wander hands-free. Take a walking stick if you need one. You will find it useful to have a brimmed hat for the sun, a small towel to sit on, and a journal to record any thoughts or inspirations. Take along a bottle of water and a snack in case you get hungry. If you are going into the wilderness, always have with you *The 10 Essentials* for safety.[37] Make it easy to be there – sufficient and unhurried, so you can be present.

Being with Nature reminds us to "stop and smell the roses." Let us take the time to enjoy the beauty of this mysterious, amazing world. Let us frolic in the trees and walk in the mountains and meadows! Relax and let go of your anxiety, your nervousness, and your impatience. Release your boredom or your overexcitement, that you may find your natural God-given balance. It is inside you, just waiting to be restored. Recalibrate!

---

[37] The Mountaineers (www.mountaineers.org/blog/what-are-the-ten-essentials).

Solitude – Being with Nature    107

Wild Rose

If you are unable to go outdoors, obtain picture books to view serene scenes of Nature from your abode. Or watch a DVD such as *Planet Earth*[38] to experience the diverse majesty and grandeur of wild places. Even without your physically being there, you can feel an energetic connection and benefit may occur.

Our inner landscape is deeply influenced by our outer landscape. Yet at the same time we learn that what is inside us influences that which is outside us; we are a unified, single system and the illusion that our being terminates with the boundary of our skin becomes apparent as we spend more time with Nature.

---

[38] *Planet Earth* (BBC Worldwide, 2007)

*Through my senses*
*the Earth may hear*
*the sweet songs of her birds,*
*feel the massage of her wind*
*through my hair,*
*and smell the fragrance*
*of her flowers and rushes.*
*Through my senses*
*She is complete.*

In silence and stillness lies the Great Mystery, the unspeakably awesome power of the universe, and the precious beauty of your own life, unfolding and flowering before your very eyes. You are it and it is you – one, together, inseparable. Within your silence and stillness is the blessed peace of communion.

After an extended time in Nature of about three or four days, I notice all the stuff I am usually thinking about has settled out and gone away, and I am way more present than before. In this solitude I am open to a wider band of reality than I operate in during my "normal" day-to-day life. At this point I then have to ask myself just what "normal" really is. Solitude in Nature awakens me and I need to have this wilderness experience regularly.

**Being with Nature offers an opportunity for us to more easily notice and develop our connections with the world around us.** Outdoors the reality of existing within the web of life becomes more apparent. This awareness predisposes us toward communication with Nature. One time in the mountains, an entire ridge of trees "got" my attention.

*The Trees That Talked*

*We speak to you now*
*as ones who, like you,*
*are much younger than*
*the mountains.*
*Sustained by the same water*
*and the same sun*
*and both blessed to be*
*in this place of wonder,*
*we have been asked to tell you*
*to share and celebrate*
*this garden with your kind.*
*The bear brings you power,*
*the deer protection.*
*We the trees, standing silently*
*in witness, give you trust.*
*The water comes and goes.*
*The animals are busy*
*on their own paths.*
*The mountains, well,*
*they have other things to do,*
*communing with the very forces*
*that created the face*
*of this earth.*
*We speak to you now as ones*
*whose lives come and go,*
*much like yours.*
*You, however, are affecting*
*how this garden grows,*
*and that is why we seek*
*your attention.*

**Solitude - Four Tips:**

1. Know where you are in Nature and take a map if you have any doubt at all. This confidence allows you to better relax and enjoy the benefits of being there.

2. Be in the natural world like you would be in a cathedral of worship. Treat the natural world like you would treat a temple. (I call it Nature Cathedral.)

3. Turn off your mobile phone, take off your watch, and allow yourself the luxury of uninterrupted communion. "Unplugging" is tremendously rejuvenating. It is not about how long you are there – it is about the quality of your experience.

4. Go barefoot. Without shoes and socks your connection with the grass, soil, sand, or ocean will allow you to benefit even more from Earth's harmonious, rejuvenating energies. This barefoot activity is called "earthing."

**Solitude - Keywords:**

Harmony, Medicine, Rejuvenation

*Chapter Eight*

# Fasting – A Higher Perception

*Fly up, up, up the ravine,
soaring,
above clouds to find
the highest resting place.
What a man dreams of,
the eagle flies above
free of dreams.
I think I hear wind below
but it could be an open mind.*

It has been well said that man cannot live on bread alone. So it is not surprising that fasting is an aspect of spiritual practice which can be highly beneficial. Denying and lightening the body so the spirit may soar is a powerful technique of purification and a tool of transformation, literally and symbolically. Because the physical aspect of being has taken on an over-weighted emphasis in our modern culture, fasting can help us recover from this imbalance.

**We need spiritual sustenance as well as the physical sustenance of food.**

The act of fasting says to Spirit, "I am here, and it is important for me to grow toward you, to be with you, to honor you and to honor myself. Let's go!" Fasting allows us to change our mind, to get off the habitual track of constant thinking which keeps us from being aware and present.

The body has so much more power than we realize. It is our plug into the power grid of cosmic energy. The body is the precious lamp, within which our universal light burns brightly. So let us be very clear that by fasting we are not at all aiming to deny our sensation of the body or lessen our value of it. While Spirit ultimately comes first, the body is our vessel, our sacred temple where transformation occurs. This is where we make our spiritual study of form, composed of earthly materials.

Fasting over a period of days puts me in a most serene state of being, where I am able to view my life from a higher perspective – from the vantage point of an Eagle soaring high above. This allows me to see the drama of my life without being caught up in it. I see myself on an epic journey and can view my habits and issues from a place of nonjudgment, and I can more easily accept myself as I am. This profound act of acceptance then leads to opportunity for real and meaningful change.

> *I am not happy*
> *and I am not sad.*
> *On the road I am watching*
> *and seeing.*
> *Things come and they go*
> *and while they are here*
> *they tremble*
> *like heat haze on the highway.*
> *The young green leaves*
> *I once called beautiful*
> *are changing.*
> *The canyon river seems*
> *to wash away my memories.*
> *I once avoided the desert*
> *and now I am here.*
> *Upon reaching the snowline*
> *on the ridge,*
> *the clouds they told me*
> *to turn around.*
> *So I am moving,*
> *discovering each moment*
> *with no wonder of what will come.*
> *No thing is more important*
> *than any other.*
> *This is Peace.*

**Consider starting with a modest fast of three days.** You can eat a few crackers each day if you are feeling too hungry or experience dizziness. You can take juice or broth to help with overall nourishment if you need to. Paramahansa Yogananda recommended fasting one day a week on orange juice in order to rest the internal organs. He also suggested fasting on orange juice two or three days in a row each month. He said this practice helps "resurrect your soul from the bad habits in eating."[39]

With a bit of experience and preparation, some people will fast for a week or more and not take anything besides water. But please remember, dear reader, this is not a contest or a competition! This is solely about what you can do (and in this case what you can do without) in order to purify yourself, in order to illuminate, grow, and come nearer to living in Spirit.

Even smaller steps, like abstaining from heavy foods such as meat for a period of time, are going to benefit you. There are juice fasts, cleansing diets, and other programs to choose from. Determine what is best for you, and always consult with a nutritionally oriented healthcare professional if you have any concerns whatsoever about the effects that may result from depriving yourself of food for a number of days.

There are various approaches to diet which can support your spiritual practice and overall health. However, the subject of diet is beyond the scope of this book, and there are many fine resources to draw from that specifically address food and the requirements of different body types. A high degree of knowledge and training is required in order to give sound advice on diet, so I shall leave it to the experts. I am simply a student who has benefited from fasting.

**When breaking a fast, do so gently.** It can be a huge shock to your system if you come off a fast with too much food too quickly, especially too much incompatible food. The first time I fasted, I did not know any better and broke it with strong

---

[39] Paramahansa Yogananda, *Journey to Self-Realization: Discovering the Gifts of the Soul* (Los Angeles, Self-Realization Fellowship, 1997).

coffee and a scone. Let me say with assurance this is not something I recommend. Be considerate to your digestive system. It will thank you.

There are other types of fasting to explore. We can approach fasting from the perspective of simplifying our lives. Letting go of those possessions or activities or habits which no longer serve us is a healthy and enlightening thing to do. We may have enjoyed and loved them greatly, yet they can become burdens for us to bear as our lives change and evolve.

Imagine you have a wonderful canoe which has taken you beautifully over the years across the lake of your life. Now, at this time of your life, you have reached the far shore and are climbing upward on Spirit Mountain. The canoe is getting very heavy, and the farther you go up the mountain, the more pain it causes you to carry it. But it is a really great canoe and you have such fond memories of good times with it. You wrestle and struggle with keeping it or leaving it, but to finally let it go gives you blessed freedom. To put the canoe down is liberating, and you are able to continue your trek more easily up the mountain of your life, toward the summit of your dreams and your destiny. Joy does not come from holding on.

Simplifying life and letting go of clutter and excess can be hard to do, but when accomplished they bring more space to your life. In that space you will grow and more easily appreciate the beauty and grace all around you. And, importantly, Spirit then has more room to participate in your life.

It is not abnormal to experience withdrawal from what we let go, just as we may from foods we stop eating. If something is eliminated from your life – whether by your direct actions or not – it is a signal that something else is on its way. It is like pruning a tree. Sometimes a big branch has to go, and it seems difficult at the time, but it always results in the type of more orderly and expansive growth you need.

> *When you find out what's worth keeping*
> *with a breath of kindness, blow the rest away.*[40]
>
> ~ Robbie Robertson

While you are fasting and simplifying your lifestyle, remember to honor your physical body – the temple wherein dwells your inner spirit. Like a tree growing from the rich soil of the Earth, so your soul grows from the riches of the body. Fasting can help you appreciate the amazing spiritual vehicle that is your physical being.

In the previous chapter we explored the value of retreating into Nature, away from the daily routines of life. I have come to experience being with Nature as an act of fasting from civilization. Retreating into the wilderness has a cleansing, purifying effect. It refreshes our minds and helps us remember what is really important to us. Being in Nature puts us in a place where we are experiencing the world around us without input from others and without being so influenced by the collective values of society. Consciously unplugging from consensual reality (the everyday reality agreed upon by the masses) is an extremely beneficial thing to do. It allows us to see our lives and this world more clearly – more as it is, rather than how we think it is.

---

[40] Robbie Robertson & The Red Road Ensemble, *Music for the Native Americans* (Capitol, 1994).

With fasting, less is truly more, but we have to be careful about getting caught up in a competitive mindset where, because we fast or pray or meditate, we believe we are better than or more spiritual than others. The moment we have this thought, we have lost our way. When this comes up, simply stop to get your bearings and regroup. We are human beings, and thoughts like these will happen. Yet we can recognize these thoughts, step back, and rebalance. Neutral acknowledgement of our flaws leads to our humble acceptance of them. Humility and acceptance are primary qualities required to walk on a spiritual path.

**Fasting - Three Tips:**

1. Check with your doctor or health professional before you begin a fast, especially if you have a medical condition.

2. Plan your fast. Begin fasting after you awaken in the morning. Many people find it easier to deal with the natural pangs of hunger this way, rather than eating breakfast and then feeling the normal hunger which comes a few hours after eating.

3. Allow yourself a cracker to stem your hunger if you are experiencing discomfort or dizziness during your fast. Sometimes just a small taste of food can ground you and put you back on your track, especially when you are first getting used to fasting.

**Fasting Keywords:**

Cleansing, Lightening, Purifying, Simplifying

## Chapter Nine

## Kindness – The Gentle Path of Joy

*I am another yourself
and you are another me.*

**There may be nothing on Earth each of us wants more from others than kindness.** When all is said and done, it is our greatest measure of a fellow human being. We may look past what we consider to be great flaws and foibles when kindness resides in the heart of another. The saying "His heart was in the right place" tells us this noble truth.

Kindness is at the very core of walking a spiritual path and living consciously in Spirit. Loving kindness toward oneself, toward others and toward the world at large can, all by itself, lead to a meaningful and fulfilling life. The simple practice of kindness will transform your life.

I really like what His Holiness the Dalai Lama says when he is asked to describe his philosophy of living and the basic essence of Buddhism. His eminently thoughtful perspective is well worth contemplating and practicing. It is paraphrased as follows:

Each of us was born, and each of us will die. Each of us has suffered, and each of us wants to be happy. We are not so different from each other. Really, we are the same. Therefore let us be kind to one another, let us be gentle with one another, let us be tolerant of one another, let us be compassionate toward one another, and let us be respectful of all life.[41] Let us try to help one another, and, if we are not able to help one another, then let us at least not hurt one another.[42]

This profound message of acceptance transcends spirituality and applies to all of us at a most basic, fundamental level. One does not have to be religious or spiritual in order to understand and practice the path of kindness. Yet kindness is a cornerstone of spiritual practice as well as human decency. Good counsel for all of us is to be like water.

---

[41] H.H. Dalai Lama & Howard Cutler, *The Art of Happiness, A Handbook for Living* (London, Hodder and Stoughton, 1998).

[42] H.H. Dalai Lama , *Overcoming Differences* (Parabola, The Magazine of Myth and Tradition, Winter 1991).

*The best of men is like water*
*Water benefits all things*
*and does not compete with them*

~ *Laotse*[43]

Each of us is on our own life path with our own unique opportunities and challenges. Each of us depends on others in order to live. Nearly all of us rely on others to provide basic functions, such as growing our food, building our homes, and making our clothing. Other people are very, very important to us. If we rely so heavily on other people, it is logical to be nice to them and to accept them as they are.[44]

**It is important to understand that the act of acceptance is not passive or weak, but is rather a conscious, active, engaging in the process of being in the world.** Kindness can be approached like an applied science that works unfailingly. The fact that kindness works gives us a practical lesson in the value of humility.

The practice of kindness teaches us much about respecting other people. It helps us understand that there is no room in this world to judge another's life path or spiritual practice. All true seekers in all religions must be honored. Mary Magdalene of the Cross teaches that each of us proceeds at our own speed on our spiritual path, and none of us are judged. She says all paths lead to portals which view the same

---

[43] Edited by Lin Yutang, *The Wisdom of Laotse* (New York, Random House, 1948).

[44] H.H. Dalai Lama & Howard Cutler, *The Art of Happiness, A Handbook for Living* (London, Hodder and Stoughton, 1998).

inner chamber.[45] This vision deserves serious contemplation. Not judging others means acknowledging, honoring and respecting them and their journey. Accepting the spiritual practices of others is a profound self-initiation.

The act of neutral acknowledgement places us squarely in the now, where we are no longer affected by our opinions of the past or our thoughts and worries about the future. This brings us to acceptance and into the ever-present, infinite realm of being where all is in harmony, and where even things which are in disharmony have their place in the grand symphony of life. Paradox is an integral part of the master cosmic score.

Concentrating on the present automatically brings more happiness. Letting go of resistance and expectation, we find joy remaining – flowering from the center of our being. Joy is our true essence, our first thought - our original face. It is what Buddhists call our Buddha nature.

> *Peace is the natural state of affairs when what's preventing it is removed.*
>
> ~ *David Hawkins*[46]

Nonviolence and nonresistance are based on a realization of the humanity of all peoples. These behavioral philosophies peel off the veneer of our thoughts and emotions and overcome our reactive conditioning in order to reveal the

---

[45] Mary Magdalene of the Cross (Temple of the Deer Wisdom School).

[46] David Hawkins, MD, Ph.D., *Power vs. Force* (Hay House, 2014).

inherent peacefulness within. As a culture, we have generally forgotten about the reality of this inner peace, but please let me assure you it is within us, protected and intact. It is awaiting an opportunity to resurface and express itself once again.

Practicing nonviolence (not harming others and not being aggressive toward them), with a genuine wish for others to be free of their suffering, is the basis of compassion. Being compassionate entails cultivating a purposeful, mindful intent, directed inward toward ourselves, which is then developed and enhanced to be shared outwardly in our interactions with others in the world. This mental attitude is based upon the value that all of us have a right to overcome suffering and be happy.[47] With compassion comes love itself, as the infinite wellspring of connection and caring we hold deep within us blossoms like a beautiful flower.

If practicing kindness and acceptance is a way to our inner being, then joy is the experience and celebration of that inner being. Joy is directly related to kindness, for what you give to others, you receive in return. Selfless acts of service, a general attitude of well-being toward others, and random acts of kindness cultivate and expose the deep connections we all share. Kindness brings nourishment to the souls of all involved in these interactions.

**Random acts of kindness are surprising gifts you bestow on others.** They are spontaneous and free-spirited without any expectation of a response, limited only by your imagination. Tell the checker at the grocery store she has a beautiful smile. Offer to give up your parking space to the car behind you. If

---

[47] H.H. Dalai Lama & Howard Cutler, *The Art of Happiness, A Handbook for Living* (London, Hodder and Stoughton, 1998).

you dial a wrong phone number, leave a message wishing the unknown recipient a nice day. Pay for the beverage of the person in line behind you at the coffee shop. Give the apple in your lunch bag to a person on the street who is asking for a handout. Give flowers to a loved one for no particular reason. Show gratitude to those you know by sending them a heartfelt, unexpected greeting card, e-mail, or phone call. Random acts of kindness bring out our best, as if a light has been shined on our goodness within. These acts help us realize more of who we really are and give us great satisfaction.

Being kind also means being good to yourself. You are good to yourself by not purposefully going against the flow and taking more stress into your life – especially about things which do not, in the end, really matter. (This, of course, is determined on a personal basis, as we all can cite different things that got us worked up, just to realize later they were not really important.) Our opinions, our righteousness, our justifications, our judgments, our forcing things, and our jumping to conclusions all bring stress into our being.

**One of the most powerful tools we have to help us in life is choice.** Sometimes, so much of what we do seems to be on autopilot. We live in routines we do not mentally interact with, but just follow without considering that we could experience life differently. And when stress and difficulty come into our lives, we forget we have options.

Choosing to be around positive music, movies, and TV shows, instead of violent, negative sounds and images can make a huge difference in how you experience life. Remember, you have a choice about how much news you take in. A low-information diet can be good for your well-being. Try choosing no TV – it's a revelation! And lest we forget one of the very best tools we have, use laughter to improve your health and sense of humor. Not taking yourself or your life too seriously is enlightening. Smiling is great for cultivating the feeling of joy. If you practice smiling like you mean it, over time you will find you are indeed feeling more joy, and you will find others more attracted to your positive, friendly energy. Fun and humor are infectious. As my nephew, Atigun, says, *"It's fun to have fun."*

Being kind to yourself includes being kind to your body. Keeping yourself fit by exercising and taking care with what you eat makes a more enjoyable life. Being kind to yourself also entails living simply. This does not mean you automatically give away all your possessions and forgo the pleasures of modern life. Rather, it is about focusing on what is really important – to live lightly enough so you can progress on your path. It is also about truly enjoying what you do have.

When you allow yourself and others to be, life becomes lighter and more enjoyable. You are not hung up on having to be right or having to judge or change anyone. It takes an incredible amount of energy to have to be right all the time, energy which is much better retained so it can be used to work for you! It is kinder and more productive to use your precious energy for self-development than it is to give it away by wasting it on judgment. If we can give up our need to be right or feel superior, we are in a favorable position to make a fundamental shift toward enjoying life in a deeper, more fulfilling way. As a byproduct, we positively affect the world around us.

Two people walking next to each other down the street may live in two entirely different worlds. One may walk in a world of peace, of joy, and harmony while the other walks in a world of violence, fear, and disharmony. What is in our inner world is reflected in our outer world. This is good news for us as we can take responsibility for the state of our inner world and guide it toward the attitudes and practices that make a life we enjoy living. Natural law (the law of correspondence) assures us this reflection – this harmony of our inner thoughts, beliefs, and attitudes with our outer actions and experiences – will inevitably occur. The ancient axiom "As above, so below" documents this eternal truth.

A positive attitude eventually begets positive experiences. Choose to be happy. Decide you are well or happy instead of unwell or unhappy, and your experience of living will begin to shift. The mind is the one thing in this world we are able to control, so let's control it! Help yourself by adopting a peaceful, kind, positive attitude. Give your inner peace a chance. Declare to yourself your happiness, and it will color and inform your life from that point onward. While it may not always be easy or simple, use the power of affirmation to help yourself. Declare you have a right to be happy!

**Could the purpose of our life be happiness?** Happy people are more loving and forgiving and sociable than unhappy people. Happy people tend to help others and positively influence the world around them. Being happy, according to the Dalai Lama, is a valid purpose in life. He teaches that enjoying a meaningful, peaceful, happy life is accomplished by developing warmth, kindness, and compassion.[48]

Writer and speaker Marci Shimoff teaches happiness techniques. Her number one happiness habit is "don't believe everything you think." Eighty percent of thoughts are negative, she says, and the habit of not believing everything

---

[48] H.H. Dalai Lama & Howard Cutler, *The Art of Happiness, A Handbook for Living* (London, Hodder and Stoughton, 1998).

we think can help us cultivate a state of peace and well-being that is not dependent on circumstances.[49]

Let the compass of your actions be guided by that which flows naturally, which comes without "pushing against the river." By accepting and dancing with the flow of life, we come into harmony with life. This does not mean all of our issues are automatically fixed and disappear, but that we begin experiencing life in a way which better serves us. And from this positive space we are able to more effectively meet our challenges.

If something is causing you stress, exasperation, or anger, consider whether you are trying to force things and, if so, back off and reflect in order to find another way through. "To yield is to be preserved whole,"[50] wrote the Taoist sage Laotse. Consider the wisdom of this approach.

Use the incredible power of choice, bolstered by courage and tempered with patience. It has been well demonstrated that you can change your life by changing your attitude toward it. People ask, "How is life treating you?" A better question is, "How are you treating life?" It is never too late for change in the realm of Spirit. Find inner harmony and you will find peace in the world, regardless of your circumstances, your physical conditions, or the state of the world at large. You will find contentment. This is how to live!

---

[49] Marci Shimoff with Carol Kline, *Happy For No Reason, 7 Steps to Being Happy from the Inside Out* (New York, Free Press, 2008).

[50] Edited by Lin Yutang, *The Wisdom of Laotse* (New York, Random House, 1948).

A Gentle Heart

**Remember to always be gentle on your path.** Be gentle with yourself and be gentle with others. To deny your responsibilities to your loved ones or your family in order to advance your spirituality is not progress. Balance is necessary in order to grow harmoniously. Whatever your responsibilities may be, know there is a way to tend to them with integrity which does not exclude anyone or anything.

Dr. Brian Alman teaches self-hypnosis to help people tap into their inner wisdom. He says the number one key element determining one's degree of happiness is by far the quality of his or her relationships. This is a scientific fact, he states.[51] You can meditate on this.

---

[51] Dr. Brian Alman (www.drbrianalman.com).

# Kindness – The Gentle Path of Joy

The gentle path of kindness is traveled by not engaging with negative thoughts or emotions. Unharmonious words and differing points of view are accepted without judgement. Accepting them is respecting them, just as you would have your words and views accepted and respected. Accepting does not have anything to do with liking or disliking what you are experiencing. Accepting is about going along with it, just as the willow bends in the heavy snow so it does not break. This approach exemplifies the middle path and the humility required to walk upon it, gained through acceptance and tolerance.

There was a time when I thought I would not be satisfied with my life unless I was a successful artist. Unless I could be financially successful making music or painting pictures, I felt emptiness within and a void I could not fill. I had unintentionally developed an underlying dissatisfaction with the quality of my life.

Eventually, when I began working with a shaman, I was able to go through a profound exercise where I identified all of the roles in my life and then let go of them gently, respectfully, one by one. After a while, I no longer defined myself by those roles and no longer identified with them as the means for how I felt about myself. No longer did I define myself as an artist, as a husband, as an employee, as a brother, as a friend, or as a son. This helped create spaciousness in my life and allowed me to more often reside in a state of equanimity. This was so empowering! But there is more, for the natural law of paradox was in play.

After this change in my life occurred, I found myself thriving, amazingly able to perform better within those roles than I had ever performed before. I could perform those functions and be in those relationships without the same attachments I felt before, without feeling I was being bound by them or defined by them. My relationships and friendships with others subsequently became deeper and more enriching. This was a fantastically liberating process.

**All of us, whether we are aware of it or not, are ultimately seeking a return to our source, to who we really are in Spirit.** This is the epic journey all souls undergo. Thus, all life paths are to be respected and honored within the space of kindness and compassion. "Do unto others as you would have them do unto you," counsels the Golden Rule. Honor is another key requirement to walk this path. *In Lak'ech,* as the Maya say: "I am another yourself," or "I am another you, and you are another me."

When Hindus and Buddhists meet in India, they often say *"Namasté."* This word, derived from Sanskrit, is a greeting as well as a parting and means "I honor that place within you where the entire Universe resides, where when you are in that place in you, and I am in that place in me, we are in the same place; we are one."[52] Put more simply, "The light in me honors the light in you," or "I respect the divinity within you that is also within me." This is what all of us really want from each other – clear, conscious, mutual acknowledgement of our own unique being.

Start from where you are. Forgive your enemies. Forgive those who have trespassed against you. Forgiving is a cleansing and purifying act. Just let it go. You don't have to give away your precious energy to the ego which has to be right, which wants to compete and have more than others do, which wants to be superior. To have to be right takes too much out of us, and we lose precious energy we simply

---

[52] Ram Dass with Stephen Levine, *Grist for the Mill* (New York, Bantam Books, 1977).

cannot afford to give away – not if we want to thrive rather than just survive. Plus, it is not our place to be right about others anyway! That is just exaggerated self-importance.

> *I can only be me – everyone else is taken.*
>
> ~ Oscar Wilde[53]

**Forgiveness is an incredibly powerful, healing form of kindness.** Accepting others and having compassion for them, we let go of our attachments and set them free. Forgiveness is also a powerful act of kindness toward ourselves as we give ourselves permission to ease the burden which has bothered us for so long. The act of forgiving brings a tremendous lightening of the load, setting us free as well. It helps quiet our mind and brings us spaciousness. Forgiveness transforms lives.

Listening to others when they speak, being fully present with an undivided attention, and releasing the need to say something of your own (the moment they finish) is another powerful practice. Not only is it an act of kindness and respect, but it teaches you to be fully present. This is like a listening meditation – taking in the words, the body language, and the context. The communication is observed with your full attention. This communion allows both of you to connect in a deeper, more profound way.

Be kind to everyone. Accept everyone. Allowing others to be who they are allows you to be who you are. Nonjudgment

---

[53] Oscar Wilde (Irish author, playright, and poet ca. 1854-1900 AD)

can be challenging to practice – but it really works!

Deer Meets Deer

**The practice of kindness may be extended beyond our relationships with people to our relationships with plants, animals, and Mother Earth herself.** All life is to be respected and honored. The bounty that we have received in order to live deserves our genuine and warm thankfulness and consideration. All of Nature that supports the deer, the lichens, the fish, the birds, the air, the water, and the trees deserves to continue existing in such a way that all of us together will be sustained.

Contemplating the deep ethics and values behind this perspective takes us beyond spiritual practice and begins to build a spiritually based philosophy impacting our ecology and even sociology and politics. We are all together in this world, unified by the fact we all depend on each other to live.

# Kindness – The Gentle Path of Joy

Even some plants and animals now depend on the loving concern of humans for their future existence, for only our consciously considerate behavior will keep them from becoming extinct.

**The practice of living in Spirit is like polishing a stone.** No matter how rough the stone may have been, with perseverance and gentle care it will eventually shine, revealing the inner beauty and divine essence which was there all along. Within each of us lies a heavenly gem, waiting patiently for us beneath the surface of our conditioning. It is ready to be handled with our lovingkindness that it may again shine radiantly and majestically, in harmony with all things in this grand and mysterious world.

**Kindness - Three Tips:**

1. While in conversation, silently think "I love you" to the other persons in the spaces before and after you speak. This activates the connection of acceptance and respect between you. Radiate love.

2. Don't be afraid to display your kindness.

3. Be like a deer, a symbol of peace in many traditions. Take only what you need and leave the rest. Learn about deer medicine.[54] Carry yourself quietly with gentleness and grace.

---

[54] The Deer is an important symbol and totem to many indigenous groups around the world. Deer medicine teaches us to embody the powers of gentleness and grace to heal ourselves and others. We move through the world as Deer, hurting no one and no thing – quiet and

## Inquire Within

**Kindness - Keywords:**

Acceptance, Gentleness, Humility, Love, Compassion

---

sensitive, yet alert and nimble, able to move decisively and quickly when necessary.

# Chapter Ten

# Artists of Life – Creating Inspiration

*Who is the man
who casts a view
a view that I have seen,
a secret as
a promise kept
through box and book
and time.*

Experiencing sacred space and the presence of Spirit is an encounter with timelessness - a taste of infinity. The act of creating art, music, or poetry has the capacity to provide this experience of expansion and unbounded existence. Artistic activity has the amazingly valuable capacity to draw out of us feelings of utter joy and glee.

Making art (and being artful) brings us into the present - the place from which our true being has never departed. Experiencing creativity takes us out of our habitual, continual train of thoughts. It is a meditation unto itself, a refresher of the mind and a tonic for the soul.

There is no agreed upon definition of art. For our purposes here we will broadly consider art to be creative self-expressions occurring in any medium. The purpose of art, as well as its cause, is subject to endless and sometimes highly charged debates which we will not engage in here. We will just say the purposes or causes of art may be inspired or uninspired. Art may be the result of focused intent, inspired by an intended aim, effect, or philosophy, or it may not. It is a fact, though, that all the art of our ancient ancestors served something. Art has always been in service to something – often to Spirit.

**Whether one's intent is to uplift the human spirit or simply to play, the creative act is filled with possibilities of healing.** Regardless of one's state of being, the creative act can provide incredibly beneficial and therapeutic effects which give us an experience of the mysterious and awesome nature of the universe we live in. This indescribable great mystery is the fountain of all creation and the signature of Spirit itself. Art can truly open one to a revelation.

## Artists of Life – Creating Inspiration

*The function of art is to reconnect the person experiencing it with their spiritual ground. It's a sort of ordering.*

~ Milo Duke

The act of creation is powerful medicine and it is easy to see why art is used as therapy. Art's ability to bring us into the timeless present removes us from the cares and worries of the day. As a young man, I used to come home from work feeling tired and stressed, unable to take my mind off my busy day. But after fifteen minutes of playing music, I had amazingly forgotten I had even been at work an hour earlier. What relief!

One moment you can be dwelling on the stress of your day, then mere moments after starting the creative process you have forgotten all about it. When you immerse yourself in creativity, worry and preoccupation gently dissolve away. Making art has the capacity to temporarily remove you from your life situation and is thus a kind thing to do for yourself and for those around you (unless art *is* your life, in which case some other practice may better assist you in your healing and self-realization). This "unplugging" also allows you to gain a new perspective on your life. Creativity can teach you how to dance with life, so you are flowing with it rather than pushing against it.

Journaling, woodworking, painting, gardening, cooking, dancing, knitting, decorating, sketching, and photography are just a few of the creative activities which can help you connect with that playful, peaceful place inside of you. Yes, skill is involved, but don't let your abilities keep you from participating in the form. Experiment! Play!

There are no rules. Just try whatever you are inclined to do, in any medium, without worrying about your level of talent. It does not matter if you haven't done it before. And it does not matter if you don't have a design, plan, or vision for your artistic undertaking. Simply playing in the artistic realm is itself a healing, rejuvenating experience of innocence and joy.

*Lay me down*
*softly on the earth*
*in a garden*
*floating by.*
*The only sound*
*must be a silent stream*
*held in by rolling greens.*

Keeping a journal gives you a place to express your feelings, to reflect, and to process thoughts and energy. I consider journaling to be an integral part of my life. Writing, as does all art, has the capacity to harmonize our inner and outer worlds.

The artistic process can also clear out unprocessed, unresolved feelings. Write with your nondominant hand and see what poetry your inner voice is waiting to express. It can be amazing what comes out once the dominant structure is bypassed. This is a powerful exercise which draws from the other side of your brain and unites the brain in wholeness. Alternatively, write letters to yourself or to others - to send or not to send as you jettison stuck, unwanted energy by expressing what you are feeling inside.

Paint a circle and intuitively add colors and shapes to create a spontaneous *mandala*, a reflection of yourself. *Mandalas* are concentric geometric shapes, configured within a circle.

Found in Hindu and Buddhist cultures, they are symbols of the universe and used as aids to meditation. Rigorously designed and created, *mandalas* are a meditative result of much training.

Rock Mandala Sand Painting

When we make our own *mandala*, it is direct evidence of who we are at that moment and what is happening in our life, as well as an evocation of our striving for the wholeness already within us. The *mandala*, an expression of self-identity, is a spiritual mirror.

**Attend to your senses and embody them.**

Let yourself dance with the music that is animating your body and inspiring your soul. Allow the creative process to just happen, without premeditation. You may be pleasantly surprised by what you create and how it makes you feel.

*Follow your bliss.*

*~ Joseph Campbell*[55]

Look at the sky and notice clouds in the shape of animals or see how the ripples of sand you walk over on the beach resemble rolling mountains as seen from an airplane high above them. You can work with dreams by recording them in a dream journal. Let go!

You might enjoy making a vision board, which can be quite an empowering process. A "planned out" vision board involves gathering together words and images, taken from magazines or elsewhere, which describe for you how you want your life to be. It can include things which affirm what is good in your life already, as well as things you want to do, places you want to go, things you want to have, or a way you want to feel. Cut or rip them to the desired shape and paste them onto a piece of poster board to form a picture of your life, as it is and as you want it to be.

---

[55] Joseph Campbell with Bill Moyers, *The Power of Myth* (New York, Doubleday, 1988).

A vision board

Or you can spontaneously make an "intuitive" vision board with no preconception whatsoever of what you are going to make. Grab a magazine, your scissors, and glue, and work rapidly, ripping, cutting, and pasting without any grand plan. Something magical and always relevant will arise as you combine images and words. All of a sudden, you realize you are bringing into the light an unspoken undercurrent – a theme or a need - running in your life. And you can now see it; it means something profound.[56]

**Ultimately, the artistic process is about connecting more deeply with your Self – about realizing wholeness.** The lands of poetry, visual art, music, and dance reside in the

---

[56] Melissa Wadsworth, *What You Notice Matters* (www.melissawadsworth.com).

world of the sacred and the soul. These soulful activities easily bridge us to the place of wholeness and beauty within. For the essence of our being is indeed beautiful. Even with all our habits and flaws, beauty resides within us. You can use art to discover your beauty. Breathe beauty. Create beauty. Be beauty.

> *Let the beauty we love be what we do.*
> *There are hundreds of ways to kneel and kiss the ground.*
>
> ~ Rumi[57]

As such, you have the option of approaching your artistic activity ceremonially, just as you would approach your altar, a temple, or a place special to you in Nature. Making art can be a conscious act of communion with Spirit. "I am here. Guide me. Help me express that part of myself that is You."

You may say, "I'm not artistic; I don't have a creative bone in my body." To you I say, with love, be an Artist of Life. Live your life artfully, elegantly, joyfully, and colorfully. Live your life with humor. Decorate your home in a pleasing manner. Express the essence of who you are through the grace of your words and deeds. That, dear reader, is what every single one of us is capable of doing: Being an Artist of Life. Just as one's entire life can become a meditation, so can one's entire life become a divine work of art. Start now. It is never too late in this world – for anyone or anything.

Art can facilitate profound realizations. Once I was sitting in my living room listening to music. Then I thought I would

---

[57] Jalāl ad-Dīn Muḥammad Rūmī (13th century Persian poet).

change the song to something more soothing and enjoyable. As the impulse to do this arose, I was overtaken by a wave of epiphany that "it is all God's music." All I would be doing is moving from one song of God's to another. With this lesson I relaxed back into my chair, sighed, and let the music keep playing.

Aside from the active experience of making art, there is also the receptive – and still participatory – experience of it, which can provide much value. Most of us have experienced this, as witnessed by the ongoing popularity of various art forms throughout history. Listening to music, viewing paintings, reading poetry, and so forth can be escapes, journeys, inspirations, and healings. These excursions can be meditations unto themselves as they take us to that timeless place within.

Using the technique of perceiving art as a singular point of concentration, one may become so absorbed in it and focused on it that the rest of the world seems to fall away. This is the same feeling garnered from the creative act itself. Here we find, though, the intent and consciousness of the creator of the art – which we cannot control – can directly affect the experience and value we derive from viewing or hearing it. Just as art can inspire feelings of joy and glee, so it can also elicit feelings of humility, horror, catharsis, and so forth.

It is important to be careful about the content of the art you take in, especially as you become more sensitive and aware. When I was a young man, undergoing what I later realized was a passage through the dark night of my soul, some very loud and oppressive music was playing. I felt it was running over me and flattening me into a dirty, dead remnant of a living being. I can only describe the experience as brutal. Then later, and most thankfully, a reprieve came like a shifting of the seasons when the music changed, and the band

*Yes* sang, "If the summer change to winter, yours is no disgrace."[58] This music – which I felt and knew in my heart at that moment to be kind music – brought me back to life. It calmed and centered me, kindly and respectfully. And it showed me that the intention of one's communications matters.

This is admittedly an extreme example of how art can affect us. What we need to understand is that subtle versions of this go on all around us in the world every single day. We are incredibly sensitive to the environment (that we are not separate from) and what we take in deeply affects us on all levels of our existence. We are much more sensitive than we realize. The world around us profoundly influences our thoughts, emotions, and physical body. And, as we are part of the environment, our physical body, thoughts, and emotions affect it as well.

As mentioned previously, you can use the power of choice regarding what imagery and energy you want in your life. Things which were once entertaining – such as graphic, violent movies, TV shows, or video games – may no longer support your growth and well-being. Endeavor to be kind to yourself and others by being considerate of the arts you choose to create and experience. Your sensitivity will reward you, protect you, and nourish you.

As we explore the various techniques of spiritual practice, we find they are parallel methods which help us create balance and harmony. These techniques work together seamlessly in virtually any combination as we artfully build our spiritual

---

[58] Yes, *The Yes Album* (Atlantic Records, 1971).

practice. Each method has in common the capacity to help us be right here, right now, where fulfillment and joy reside.

Spiritual practice is, by definition, a conscious practice. We help ourselves by being aware and not forcing the process. This is the exact opposite of making up our mind and forcing things, which is being less conscious.

Dear reader, let us trust that in the big picture it is not possible to make a mistake. What we call our wrong turns and bad choices, even if they are painful, provide us with lessons we learn from for a lifetime. And if we can see these challenging experiences through the eyes of gentleness and compassion, then our character will grow, and our wisdom will mature beyond our years.

**Art - Three Tips:**

1. Don't worry in the slightest how your artistic effort will look, sound, or read. Just do it and enjoy the process. No one is judging you. Be gentle with yourself.

2. Check out or buy a book on whatever creative subject you are interested in. If it is something you have been curious about for some time, all the better. Make time to read it and see what happens, without any intended outcomes.

3. Take an art class. You can learn some basic painting techniques, for example, or find a class in playing the guitar or whatever else you are curious about or feel drawn to.

**Art - Keywords:**

Creativity, Expression, Play

*Chapter Eleven*

# Ancient Wisdom – Tapping Deep Roots

*Seek the quiet places
that you may hear the mysteries...
That the echoes of the ancients
will rise in you...
We are here, we are here
and so are you...
Go now and shine brightly
with our Light...*

Why should we care about the Maya, the Pygmy, or the Inuit? Is there anything we can learn from the Q'ero, the Native American, or the Aboriginal People? What values and perspectives on life might they hold that we can benefit from?

The answers to these questions are relevant to us in this time of personal and planetary need.

The trees give us oxygen to breathe and help create the nourishing rains upon which we depend, sustaining life. There is less rain in places where the trees have been cut down or burned. Erosion and drought are hastened. Fires begin which Nature can no longer extinguish. For the Maya, trees are intermediaries between the physical and spiritual worlds and absolutely essential to life. They believe that without the tree, man cannot survive. "With the death of the last tree comes the death of the human race."[59]

**There is a great deal we can learn from the indigenous peoples who preceded our modern civilization and who still live aplenty on this fine planet.** An indigenous culture, at its core, values the relationship humans have with the Earth, with the Sun, and with Spirit, and these values direct their way of being.

Living through the changes and uncertainties of these modern times is like being in the middle of a cosmic storm. In such conditions one needs to have deep roots in order to survive and prosper, and the indigenous peoples' ways and spirituality have those deep roots, anchoring them into the Earth and the web of life. Our ancestors have practical living skills developed over a very long period of time which have proven themselves by the virtue of their continued existence. Tapping into a strong, well-established tradition supports us

---

[59] Cynthia MacAdams, Hunbatz Men, Charles Bensinger, *Mayan Vision Quest, Mystical Initiation in Mesoamerica* (HarperCollins Publishers, 1991).

during challenging times and helps us stay grounded and energized in the swirling winds of accelerating change.

We can also learn from indigenous people how to live in harmony with each other and with the Earth and discover how they experience their connections with Spirit. We may come from different families and traditions, but all of us share the same ancestors. Ancient wisdom is here for all humankind to learn and benefit from, with great gratitude and respect.

Much ancient knowledge has been purposely hidden for centuries due to persecution or extermination at the hands of invading conquerors who stole and settled the indigenous peoples' lands. But now the Maya, the Q'ero, and many others believe all of us urgently need this wisdom in these crucial times. Mayan shaman and daykeeper Elder Hunbatz Men eloquently stated this when he told Lisa and me, "To be Mayan is not the color of your skin. To be Mayan is your consciousness."

I would like to tell you the story of the Mayan marriage ceremony that Hunbatz Men performed for Lisa and me in Mexico. It illustrates the benefits of learning about and experiencing the ancient ways. On Winter Solstice 2004, this was a celebration of twenty years of civil marriage. We were originally wed by a Justice of the Peace in a Seattle courthouse, and eventually we both desired to have a spiritual ceremony.

Seven of us arrived at the Temple of *Ak'e* in the Yucatan in mid-morning under a brilliant sun. Joining Lisa and me were Lisa's mother, Maureen; Mary Magdalene of the Cross and her friend Mary; Hunbatz Men and his friend, William, a Mayan archaeological expert. No one else, except for the gentleman we purchased our admission from, was there at

*Ak'e*. Hunbatz Men, who is from the *Itza* Maya tradition, sat us down on the bottom step of the main temple in the shade of the lone tree along its wide base.

James, Lisa, and Hunbatz Men at the Temple of *Ak'e*

He proceeded to speak with us for a long while, educating us about the history of the Mayan people living in this particular area, and telling us about the Mayan wedding ceremony – what it means and what the responsibilities are of those who engage in it. It was like a Mayan university lecture on marriage.

Hunbatz Men said a Mayan marriage may occur when two human beings have each reached the ends of their individual roads, their paths, and they are ready to walk together on a new path. The Mayan concept of marriage is very different from the Western world's view, in which the society is run for and controlled by men. To the Maya, men and women are equal, and the world needs counsel from both of them. The man could be "scared of the trees," and the woman could help him with it. The woman could be "afraid of the night," and the man could help her with that. Life is approached and experienced together.

Hunbatz Men told us our marriage would also be with the air, the wind, the trees, the stones, and the sun. If we were to decide no longer to be together, he did not want a phonecall or letter from us – rather, we would have to tell the air, the wind, the trees, the stones, and the sun. This way of being adds great depth to the idea of marriage as we know it in Western civilization.

For the Maya, marriage is with the whole world – with all the elements, with each other, with the Cosmos, and with *Hunab K'u*,[60] the Only Giver of Movement and Measure.[61] Marriage brings with it a responsibility to help create a better world, to live in a new way – which is really an old, time-tested way.

Hunbatz Men led us to the far side of the long grassy plaza extending south from the temple. We arrived at a stela (a standing stone symbolizing the sacred tree), set prominently by itself. He counseled us there and made prayers to Father

---

[60] Carlos Barrios (Sedona, Prophets Conference, 2004). Mayan daykeeper Carlos Barrios said that *Hunab K'u* is a Mayan name for God. *Hun* is one, *Ab* is diversity, and *K'u* is heart. Therefore *Hunab K'u* means "the diversity of one unity in one heart." (Father Sun is our local representative of *Hunab K'u*.)

[61] Hunbatz Men, Secrets of Mayan Science/Religion (Santa Fe, Bear & Company, 1990). According to Hunbatz Men, *Hunab K'u* symbolizes form and energy and is the Absolute Being, the architect of our universe. *Hunab K'u*, the giver of movement and measure, is represented symbolically by a square within a circle.

Sun and Mother Earth. He asked that we be taken care of and made happy. It was such a beautiful, touching, heartfelt prayer.

Following his instructions, we waited until he slowly walked back to the main temple and ascended the giant steps to meet our small wedding party. Then Lisa and I proceeded slowly, stopping many times on our procession. During the entire extended, slow-motion walk toward and up onto the Temple of *Ak'e*, Hunbatz Men blew a high-pitched bone whistle, a whistle that seemed to conjure the wind.

The wind came up suddenly and blew strongly from behind us. We felt the wind pushing, guiding, and inspiring us upwards. We remembered our instructions as we walked, communing with the elements and putting our negative thoughts and experiences into the Earth. Mother Earth accepts them from us, Hunbatz Men told us; she takes our burdens when we give them to Her. It was an emotional walk with tears of joy.

We arrived at the top of the magnificent temple to an awesome panorama and stood side by side in front of Hunbatz Men. Lisa held out her left hand and I held out my right hand and Hunbatz Men bound them together with a colorful woven cloth band. Then tobacco was placed in those hands, and we were told to close our eyes.

Hunbatz Men made a prayer in Mayan and then in English. At one point he had Lisa open her right eye and held a quartz crystal upon it. Then he had me open my left eye and held the crystal upon it. Then he stood behind us, our eyes closed again, and blew the bone whistle several times in succession.

During this sequence I experienced two powerful sensations. First, I saw a vision of us being married at the top of a different Mayan temple – one I have never seen in this lifetime – in a similar style of ceremony with similar Earth and sky around us. We have done this before, I realized.

The second sensation was – with Lisa's right eye opened and my left eye opened, and with the shrill whistle blowing through us – we had become a single body, bound together and animated by the whistle.

**Hunbatz Men told us to be happy, that a happy body makes a happy spirit, and a happy spirit makes a happy body. He told us it is very important to help each other to be happy by smiling.** What beautifully simple and practical advice!

We opened our eyes, and he unbound us and sent us to opposite sides of the temple's long platform to deposit our tobacco as an offering. With that done, we met back in the middle, and the ceremony was complete. Pictures were taken, and we descended the grand steps to leave the sacred grounds after this profound and blessed ceremony on this special solstice day.

A week later we were in Palenque, visiting the temples there again and reuniting with friends. When I found Pedro López and told him about our experience in *Ak'e,* he revealed what *Ak'e* means to his people. In Pedro's native *Chol* Maya language, *Ceh* (pronounced kay) is Deer. *A* (pronounced Ah) is Temple. "Ah," he said, is the sound one makes in response to communion with God, with Spirit, with that which is so great that words cannot communicate the awe, the power, and the largeness of It. *Ak'e,* Temple of the Deer...incredible![62]

---

[62] This was notable for me, personally, as 1) I already had an association with Deer as a primary totem and teacher; 2) Pedro Lopéz revealed on a

**Putting Spirit first is the beginning of living right.** All else follows from this starting point. This is not superstitious mumbo-jumbo or blind hopefulness, but a scientifically documentable fact as evidenced by those successful cultures which have lived this way. We can define a successful culture as one which has endured on this Earth for a very long time. It seems the ability of our modern culture to be successful in this way is being tested at this time.

> *We are all*
> *placed on this Earth*
> *for a purpose.*
>
> ~ *Yakama Nation*[63]

Look at all the countries and civilizations we have studied in our history books. They come and they go. Some last for 200 or 300 or more years; many of them last for less. Our indigenous ancestors, the tribes which exist in nearly every corner of the world, have roots going back thousands of years. They have existed continuously while many more recent civilizations have come and gone. It is precisely these traditions which have the knowledge and wisdom about how we can sustain ourselves on this planet.

**A healthier planetary culture starts with each of us as individuals.** If you are bringing Spirit into your life, whether

---

previous trip to Palenque (Chiapas, Mexico) that Palenque means "House of the Deer" in Chol Maya; and 3) I had, at that point, already been studying for six years within Temple of the Deer Wisdom School.

[63] Yakama Nation Cultural Museum, quotation displayed, Toppenish.

it is via an earnest desire to move forward on your path or whether you are in crisis or distress and are responding to change, then you are in the right place right now to do what you need to do.

And if you are in a place on your life path where you need assistance, then I highly recommend you consider working with a shaman. A shaman can help you heal and help you find the path to your destiny.

Shamanism is the oldest healing practice we have on planet Earth. This is because it works. Working with the luminous energy field of your body, with your *Chi*, a shaman can bring you into balance and alignment with yourself. And this work can be accomplished in an amazingly short period of time – in many cases within days, weeks, or months versus years and years via modern therapeutic methods.

Shamanistic healing has the capacity to cut straight to the heart of the issues at hand, including how we process physical pain, emotional trauma, or psychic wounds. A shaman can journey to find parts of ourselves that may we may have hidden away in order to cope with intense, life-altering events, in this lifetime or in past lifetimes. Indigenous peoples from all parts of the globe have shamans who are known locally as healers, curanderos, medicine men, or medicine women, and who can aid us immensely in our personal journey because they are holders of the vast repository of ancient wisdom.

Ancient wisdom is here to assist us in both personal and planetary healing and transformation. Ancient wisdom is Earth medicine, humanity's original translations of the workings of the Universe into a holistic practice of integrated science, spirituality, and healing art. Meditation, prayer, chanting, dance, and divination are among the techniques used by our ancestors. These techniques are as valid today as they were millennia ago.

Divination is the art of acquiring occult, or hidden, knowledge. Various forms of divination have arisen in different places around the globe. The *I-Ching*[64] from China is a prime example of a divinatory tool. You can use divination to gain clarity, for a reality check, or for illuminating a deeper understanding of an issue you are dealing with. Tools of divination allow us to consult with our higher self, with the totality of our being, which includes Spirit. In this way we use more than our thinking, rational mind and access that place within us where infinity and harmony exist. From this place comes wisdom on how to look at an issue or how to work through it.

Depending on the tradition, coca leaves, seeds, twigs, and other earthy matter is used for divination. More recent forms of these ancient tools include runes and divinatory decks of cards such as tarot. You may find one of these systems works for you. The patterns and constellations formed by divination tell us things. It is very personal, and because each of us has powerful intuition – whether we know it or not – we can develop the capacity to use divinatory tools.

**Our great ancestors were acutely aware of the natural cycles of time involving the rhythms of the Earth, Sun, and Moon, as well as those of the major planets and stars.** They lived their lives informed by and in accordance with these cycles. One of the simple, effective ways we can access ancient wisdom is by tracking the cycles of the Moon and the

---

[64] The *I-Ching* (translated as "Book of Changes" or "Classic of Changes") is an ancient Chinese text long used as an oracle and divinatory tool.

rhythms of Earth's orientation to the Sun – namely, the Equinoxes and the Solstices.

We are in tune with lunar rhythms, for example, when we use a calendar showing the phases of the moon to choose when to plant a garden or when we consult a tide chart to go fishing. This awareness moves us toward harmony with the Cosmos, which, in turn, puts us in position to tap into the wisdom accumulated by those who practiced this way of being before us. New moons are favorable days for new beginnings, for plantings, for beginning new projects, and for the seeding of what will become. Full moons are days for celebration and giving thanks for what has increased, what has grown, and what has been gained.

We can also access ancient wisdom by keeping calendars older than the Gregorian calendar which dominates our modern world. The Gregorian calendar, while it is a useful tool, is not a harmonic system of keeping time. It has been argued our modern calendar bears some responsibility for the increasingly frenetic and fast-paced changes we are undergoing on planet Earth - changes which we are seemingly unable to keep up with on a personal level.[65]

What if the Moon cycles were different lengths – some 28 days and some 30 or 31 days? It is highly likely the physical dissonance and chaos would disrupt and even destroy the natural cycles of life which flow only in evenly proportioned rhythms. At some level there may be unhealthy effects from our unevenly proportioned Gregorian calendar system. It is

---

[65] José Argüelles, Ph.D., *Time & the Technosphere, The Law of Time in Human Affairs* (Rochester, Bear & Company, 2002).

like having a ruler with inches of uneven length – something that does not make sense to create, let alone use.

The Mayan calendar is a valuable way to access the nature of time from a different perspective than what we are used to. There is a certain elegance and artistry to the Mayan sacred calendar called the *Tzolkin*. This "Book of Days" consists of thirteen numbers and twenty daysigns which combine into 260 permutations - 260 different days before the cycle begins again. The *Tzolkin* cycle, one of many Mayan cycles which harmoniously interlock, runs and repeats continuously. So 260 days from now will bring up the exact same combination of number and daysign as today. Therefore the Mayan number and daysign assigned to the day you were born recurs every 260 days. This day is your Mayan birthday, a day of power which resonates deeply for you. There are websites on the Internet which will convert your Gregorian birth date into the corresponding Mayan *Tzolkin* date.[66] Tracking your ceremonial birthday is interesting and enlightening.

Just as the seven days of our week have different qualities, so the twenty Mayan daysigns have different energies as well. Eagle, Death, and Wind are three of the daysigns, each with their own opportunities. For example, Eagle is a day to celebrate and ask for abundance. Death is a day to honor and connect with ancestors. Wind days help us connect with Spirit, the breath of life. Each of the thirteen numbers has specific qualities, too. There is much depth to plumb if connecting with this alternative calendar rhythm calls to you.

Fellow initiate Roger Aldridge wrote to me on this subject and I shall let his words speak for themselves. "The Mayan cycles are alive and part of life itself. They express a

---

[66] The Mayan Calendar Portal (www.maya-portal.net/tzolkin).

continuum of the vast hugeness of the Cosmos and small aspects of physical life. If this is true, then these cycles have been occurring from the earliest times on this planet and were not 'invented' by a particular culture – anymore than acupuncture meridians in the body were invented by the Chinese."[67]

Temple of Inscriptions, Palenque, Mexico

In 2004, Carlos Barrios, a shaman and daykeeper from Guatemala representing the Mayan elders, spoke in Sedona, Arizona.[68] He said the first lesson of the elders is that it is easy for us to lie to ourselves. We must start here, where we are, and be honest with ourselves, he said. We must ask ourselves

---

[67] Roger Aldridge (letter to author, 2009).

[68] Carlos Barrios (Sedona, Prophets Conference, 2004).

if we are doing the best to work for change, to plant a seed of consciousness in others.

Mr. Barrios said that while it is good to meditate, we also need to act. We need to stop the destruction of the environment in a big way, and the only thing the elders ask of us at this time is that we take action. If we don't, the dark forces of materialistic power will destroy humanity and the environment. As Mr. Barrios explained it, the dark forces are very organized and know exactly what they want – to maintain the current materialistic power structure at all costs, even if it means destruction. But the light forces – the light workers – all have their own ideas about what the best action is to take; they are not organized or coordinated. The light workers pick and choose from traditions but need to honor the whole tradition, he said. We must learn how to negotiate and save Mother Earth, for She wants us to create peace and balance.

Carlos Barrios's *Book of Destiny: Unlocking the Secrets of the Ancient Mayans and the Prophecy of 2012*[69] is an extraordinary and relevant resource. As a tool to help us understand our life purpose and excel during our time on Planet Earth, I highly recommend it.

A convention which many of our ancestors share is that of three worlds, oriented vertically, which make up what is known as the World Tree, the Sacred Tree, and the Tree of Life, or the Axis Mundi. In this model there is the interior underworld with Nature spirits, a central or middle world of matter where we physically live, and an upper world of

---

[69] Carlos Barrios (translated by Lisa Carter), *The Book of Destiny: Unlocking the Secrets of the Ancient Mayans and the Prophecy of 2012* (New York, HarperOne, 2010).

spiritual beings. Shamans work with helping spirits in the upper and lower worlds to aid in the healing process. The tree of life is a motif common to many traditions that symbolizes the interconnection of life on our planet.

In some traditions, the mythic tree of life is also related to the Milky Way. This brings in the ancient concept of the world age, also called the Great Year or the Platonic Year. It is approximately 25,800 years in duration, the length of the zodiacal cycle. In Western astrology we are now in transition from the Age of Pisces into the Age of Aquarius. This great cycle of time was discovered by all our significant ancestor cultures – among them the Egyptians, the Greek, the Chinese, and the Maya. It is the length of the Precession of the Equinoxes, calculated empirically by our ancestral astronomers.[70] The Mayan calendar is connected to this great cycle.

**You can also tap into the vibrations of ancient cultures by visiting the sacred sites they venerated in so many places around the world.** These ancient temples, mounds, stone circles, and natural rock formations awaken that part of us which is beyond time. Let us remember that everything is made of energy, and our own luminous energy field can go into harmonic resonance with people, with places, and with the planet. Within this resonance lies our natural state of balance, with ourselves and with the Universe.

Many sacred sites were used, or even designed, for the high purpose of causing awakening and transformation through communion and ceremony. Hopefully the governments and institutions which control many of these world treasures will

---

[70] John Major Jenkins, *Maya Cosmogenesis 2012* (Santa Fe, Bear & Company, 1998).

one day allow the ritual activities they were designed for to be performed there once again – for the benefit of all.[71]

Uluru, Australia

Sacred sites are the natural altars of the Earth - places to make offerings, places to give thanks, to make prayers, practice meditation, and so forth. Inspired and informed by Spirit, these places can give you a tremendous charge. Go to them. Be with them. Be inspired. These are profoundly powerful spots on our grand planet. Some say these places are Earth chakras – nodes of energy within the luminous body of the Earth itself. We draw power from these places and we also energize them with our presence to create more of the peace

---

[71] The wishes of the traditional guardians of a sacred site may need to be honored as to whether making ceremonies there is appropriate.

and awakening that we need so much, personally and planetarily.

Many traditions have been sharing spiritual information with initiates through mystery or wisdom schools. These schools train earnest initiates in ancient ways and customs, incrementally guiding them through increasing levels of learning. As the information being taught is occult or hidden knowledge, only after each level is processed and integrated does the initiate move to the next level.

If you work with an ancient tradition, hopefully you can have an opportunity to experience and benefit from some of the ceremony within it. Ceremony is not only how traditions stay alive, but ceremony is the mythical backbone of the lineage. Individuals come and go over the years, but ceremony is an enduring constant. Ceremony is the hub around which the wheel of life turns. Ceremony is so important and enriching that I have dedicated an entire chapter to it, coming up next.

**Ancient Wisdom: Three Tips:**

1. Learn about the people indigenous to the place where you grew up or live now. How did they live? What did they believe? What were their traditions? Who were their healers? What might you have already learned from them? What do you want to learn from them?

2. Select a place in the world which has always fascinated you. Learn about the indigenous peoples who inhabit or who formerly inhabited it. What draws you there? What are their traditions? What might you be able to learn from them?

3. Contemplate the ancients who healed people with plants, who built pyramids perfectly aligned to the heavens, and who developed the techniques of meditation. What did they believe? What did they value? What can you learn from them to apply to today's challenges, personally and planetarily? What do you have in common with them?

**Ancient Wisdom - Keywords:**

Ancestor, Lineage, Ceremony

## Chapter Twelve

## Ceremony – Bringing it all Together

*Thank you, thank you, thank you,
thank you, thank you.*

Many of us are feeling that the world is speeding up – that things are happening faster and faster. It seems change is occurring ever more rapidly as time goes by. While perhaps some of this can be attributed to a relative perception of the days and years going by more quickly as we get older, there does indeed seem to be something about this acceleration of change.

There are many reasons to do ceremony. One of them is to balance the sensation of the speeding up of life with the timeless experience of ceremony, of being in sacred space. The faster things go, the more ceremony is needed to keep up with the energies required. "Ceremony, ceremony, ceremony," was the counsel that Falcon Medicine Woman Diana Falconi gave to me.

**"A ceremony is an activity, infused with ritual significance, performed on a special occasion."**[72] Ceremonies are traditionally made on such occasions as Solstices, Equinoxes, New and Full Moons, birthdays, wedding anniversaries, inaugurations, coronations, and on religious holy days. A ceremony has significance because we decide it does. We deliberately marry intention with action and find ourselves walking the ancient path of ritual. This path of wholeness brings us into the now, with its opportunities for healing and freedom.

The type of ceremony I wish to speak of involves being in a space outside our normal day-to-day life and outside of consensual reality (the everyday reality agreed upon by the masses). It involves a conscious intent to connect with Spirit, or some aspect of Spirit such as Father Sun or Mother Earth, and it connects with that part of us that is Spirit. Ceremony is no less than a ritual to come into harmony with the Universe and to recognize oneself as being a part of Nature and its cycles – the lunar, planetary, and solar rhythms which inform us, grow us, and inspire us.

In this Spirit-filled framework, the Earth is alive, the Sun has a mind, and the Galaxy has desires. This sets the table for any of the spiritual practices presented in this book to be

---

[72] Wikipedia

conducted in a ceremonial manner. But let's go deeper. We can we weave together several practices into a meaningful program, whether it is conducted spontaneously or is planned out ahead of time.

**Timing ceremonies to Nature's cycles allows them to be magnified by the naturally energetic qualities of auspicious days.** You may find detailed information in the Appendix on when certain celestial days of interest occur within the Gregorian calendar over the coming years.

On a summer Solstice some years ago I was given specific instructions by spiritual teacher Mary Magdalene of the Cross, involving going to a place in Nature where I could see the sun rise on Solstice morning. I parked at the end of a logging road in the eastern reaches of the Cascades mountains in Washington State and hiked uphill two miles in the dark to a place that, on the map, seemed to have an unobstructed view to the east. I barely slept in my sleeping bag in the cold meadow under a sea of stars. Around 4 a.m., when the sky began to lighten, I sat up and shivered to watch the light play on the distant horizon. As Father Sun arose, I stood and stared deeply into Him to receive the message I was told to go out and receive.

This was a simple ceremony. It involved going to a place of power on an auspicious day, feeling grateful for being there, and being open to a new vision I had prayed to receive. The experience thrilled and fulfilled me in ways I cannot describe. I have gone back to that panoramic vista periodically to observe summer solstice, and it grows in power for me with each visit. Being there nourishes my soul. It is important to note that I do not at all advise you to stare at the sun. By all counts this is a dangerous act to perform.

Summer Solstice Sunrise

**A full blown ceremony can involve a lot of ritual.** There may be fasting and then, when the day of ceremony occurs, the washing of one's body, a literal and symbolic cleansing and purification. There may be dressing in a particular manner – perhaps ceremonial whites augmented with jewelry and stones. In this way we honor Spirit and we honor ourselves as emissaries of Spirit. And we acknowledge and magnificently magnify our intent.

Opening sacred space by honoring the directions brings us into the place where ceremony can occur safely and in a deeper, more meaningful manner. Meditation then calms and slows down the mind so the whole process may be honored and appreciated more fully. Making a prayer or an offering further opens the great space of peace and joy wherein ceremony and our Spirit thrive. For detailed information on opening and closing sacred space, refer to Alberto Villoldo's excellent book, *Shaman, Healer, Sage*[73]

> *Late evening I bathe*
> *slowly*
> *don my ceremonial whites*
> *gently*
> *light the altar candles*
> *fire the sage and take it slow*
> *around the four walls*
> *and four limbs*
> *the head and deeply*
> *I breathe the smoke*
> *the scent,*
> *the quiet*
> *gentle peace, sit down and*
> *unwrap sacred stones*

We benefit by using the tools we have in our spiritual tool bag more fully by being more effective in our preparation and intent. There is something deeply magical about focusing intention and magnifying it through the powerful lens of ceremony. This puts us in direct alignment with Spirit. As we were created by Spirit, all that Spirit has, we have as well. Ceremony can align us with the energy of this truth.

---

[73] Alberto Villoldo, Ph.D., *Shaman, Healer, Sage: How To Heal Yourself and Others with the Energy Medicine of the Americas* (New York, Harmony Books, 2000).

Flower Offering

One type of ceremony simply involves a way of being, rather than any specific outward actions. For example, we may have a friend who is going through some ordeal. We can choose to assist them in a nonattached way by "holding space." Being present in these situations, in a state of nonjudgment, able to interact as we may be asked to, but not planning any intervention, puts us in a place of resonance and support where we are able to "be there" (hold space) for them in a very healthy way. We are in a safe place because we are not forcing our involvement, yet we are helping by creating a regal, stable, gentle peace around and even within our friend.

The key to holding space is not to take other people's stuff on, for we are not responsible for them. We can rather witness and simply let it be. This is a way into the path of compassion. We can hold space for people who are in need or who are ill, imagining the best for them, providing unconditional love and just being there in a supportive, nonmeddling way that assists and facilitates them to work with their own energy in a nonthreatening environment.

As I write these words on the eve of Winter Solstice, I am reminded of the longstanding tradition of burning candles or keeping a fire going all Winter Solstice night. This is done in hope and in trust that the light will overcome the darkness and the Sun will return to lighten our lives. It is also a metaphor for the inner light of our Spirit overcoming the darkness and doubt of our lives. The Solstices, Equinoxes, and their midpoints are auspicious times for ceremony, as are New Moons and Full Moons. Full Moon Fire Ceremonies are a regular part of the Andean Q'ero tradition, used to power our dreams, release what we have outgrown, and to give great thanks.

Winter Solstice, since the majority of Earth's people live in the Northern hemisphere, is the most celebrated time of the year. Also known as Yule or Midwinter, Winter Solstice holiday is older than and central to Christmas. This time of darkness, the womb of Winter, is a time to make changes and new beginnings, and it is a time of celebration. People around the world gather together in groups to feast and give gifts. This leads to the New Year and its opportunities for a fresh start, for making commitments to a better, brighter future.

Making offerings in a ritualistic way is a solid basis for ceremony. As all things contain Spirit, which is consciousness, the Sun and the Earth are themselves living beings, albeit very large ones. They greatly affect us and we affect them, too. Ceremony awakens us to commune with the Universe in a most empowering way.

Prayer used in ceremony is tremendously powerful. Here is a prayer Mary Magdalene of the Cross gave a group of us located in different parts of the world for a Summer Solstice ceremony. Ceremonies which roll across time zones are like a wave, gaining momentum as they build. When we think of the people participating, before us in the East and after us in the West, it adds energy to the experiences of all involved.

*Oh Tonantzin, Goddess of Earth and Spring and Maize*
*I thank you for what you have done for me*
*you have helped me in so many ways.*
*You have made a path for me to walk in*
*help me to walk in it.*
*Help me to continue*
*give me strength and courage.*
*There is so much I have done against you,*
*by my fathers,*
*forgive me, forgive them.*
*You have given me so much,*
*I've only taken – never giving back,*
*forgive me, forgive them.*
*Now I stand in your presence*
*willing to return all that has been taken.*
*Goddess of goodness and compassion,*
*I give myself to you in return.*
*Take me back into your nurturing arms,*
*there is no other reason for life*
*but that I return to you all that I have taken;*
*it is I, it is I, it is I.*
*In this way may I always stand ready to serve you*
*Goddess of Earth and Spring and Maize.*
*In this age of feminine energy*

*never allow me to forget you again.*[74]

There are many opportunities for ceremony within the many traditions of our world. In the end, for us to be in tune with ourselves, happy with our lives, and in accord with Spirit, we just simply need to do our work. For if we don't do our work and everyone else does theirs, we are still missing a crucial piece in the great puzzle of creating a new world: ourselves.

**May you do whatever you do with sincerity and intent, with the goal of weaving all the varied aspects of your life into a way of being that energizes and nourishes you.** May you be inspired by the path you choose to walk, that has heart and that fulfills you. This is indeed the blessed ceremony of your life. Enjoy, enjoy, enjoy.

*Aum, Peace, Amen.*
*May the Blessings Be -*
*Everything is as it should be.*

### Ceremony: Three Tips

1. Plan your ceremonies ahead of time so you can prepare for them. Setting aside uninterrupted time dedicated just for ceremony and being in a suitable state of mind significantly raise their effectiveness.

---

[74] Mary Magdalene of the Cross (Temple of the Deer Wisdom School, reprinted with permission).

2. Mark the upcoming Solstice and Equinox dates on your calendar over the next year. Resolve to make a ceremony in observance of these four key Earth holidays occurring annually. This will plant a seed which will grow as you imagine, prepare for, and make the ceremonies.

3. Join with a group in your area for a ceremony. Use this opportunity to expand your ideas of what ceremony can be like and to explore and benefit from the power of group mind.

**Ceremony - Keywords:** Ritual, Intention, Significance

## Chapter Thirteen

## Living in Spirit

*At the top of the mountain*
*All directions call*
*But I know the way*
*To go*

*Within, the inner lamp alights*
*The path to peace*
*And understanding*
*Growing in the garden*
*Of the soul*

*In the pool of interior reflection*
*Awaits the face*
*Of grace and harmony*

**Let us underscore a key point of this book. Spiritual practice is our individualized way of learning to live in the ever-present now, the place where healing and harmony reside.** A spiritual practice includes any activity that cultivates awareness of the presence of Spirit in our lives.

In previous chapters we explored a variety of ways you can create more peace and joy in your life. Now that you have had a chance to choose one or two or more of the techniques we have explored to work with, it is time to complete the circle by taking your new way of being into the world. It is time to humbly take your show on the road.

**Yes, it is beneficial to learn how to meditate or how to pray, but we still have jobs to do, children to raise, dinners to cook, and love to make.** Taking what we learn on our spiritual path and integrating it with the rest of our lives – which are not at all separate from our spirituality – is where the rubber meets the road. Each whole life is an opportunity for growth and transformation when we focus bravely through the lens of living in Spirit.

We want to practice kindness. Are we being kind at the office, in the check-out line, and at home? We want to live in gratitude. Are we thankful for our food, for our friends, for our coworkers, for each day? How we treat those closest to us is the best indicator of our progress in life. The quiet solitude found and nurtured within our spiritual practice is very sustaining, but it is enhanced and made complete by our ongoing interaction with the fantastic, multidimensional, interconnected, and interdependent world around us.

"Be Here Now." These simple words of wisdom from Ram Dass[75] embody the archetype of grounding, centering, and connecting deeply with the Cosmos - advice that serves us so very well in everything we do. In this way we are present, aware, and participating willfully in both the sorrows and joys of life. We energize ourselves by allowing all aspects of our lives to feed us, to nourish us, and to teach us the grand mysteries of existence within this unspeakably awesome and beautifully strange universe – a universe we share with the stones, the plants, the animals, the stars, and the angels and avatars who are guiding and inspiring us from beyond the dimensions of time and space.

Let us have faith. May we be blessed that we can do this thing called life in such a way that we suffer less and feel happier more often. By committing to an attitude that "Spirit is within me and I can do this!" we access a deeper level of energy – a supply that is inexhaustible, fed by the same source that moves the Earth and powers all the heavens.

Faith is key to living in Spirit. Faith helps us live meaningful, purposeful lives. As we do those things which move us toward our higher goals and purposes, we find balance and harmony, and our faith deepens. Faith feeds action which feeds more faith. All feeds all in the circle of life, and, as we plug into this spiraling circuit of cosmic energy, we find our stride. It is not about achieving but about realizing and being who we really are.

**Go forth and prosper! Sit still and prosper! Go to your job or your dinner, be with your child or your lover, and trust that the new way you are being will burn brightly like the Sun, shining through the fog to illuminate peace and love**

---

[75] Ram Dass, *Be Here Now* (Hanuman Foundation, 1971).

**in your life.** You are a divine, radiant being, and, as you allow your essence to come forth, you will deeply affect your life and the lives of those around you. Proceed with the confidence you have earned and deserve! Let your radiance shine and light the way for you to walk your path with love, in harmony, in peace. It is your birthright.

**Practice is the process that transforms your intention into results.** Whether you are drawn to prayer, meditation, or some other spiritual vehicle, with my full and grateful heart I encourage you to practice. With will and perseverance you already have within you the power you need to live a joyful, satisfyingly creative life. Yes, spiritual practice does take discipline, yet the very act of practicing creates this discipline. Know that your practice will deepen naturally the further you go into it.

*Your life is your spiritual practice.*

Whatever you do, and at whatever speed you choose to do it, be sincere, have fun, and embrace the process. All of us need to remember to laugh at times and not take the drama so seriously. The spiritual way is found in lightness, grace, kindness, gratitude, and humor. It is found by sending our roots deep into the Earth that we may be well anchored for the expansion and transformation of our being.

All the formal techniques of spiritual practice are like lattices upon which your soul may grow upward toward its undeniable source in Spirit. And one day even this lattice, the very structure of your practice, will be left behind as you soar into the heavens wing to wing with the Great Spirit.

*Appendix One*

# Moon, Solstice & Equinox Data

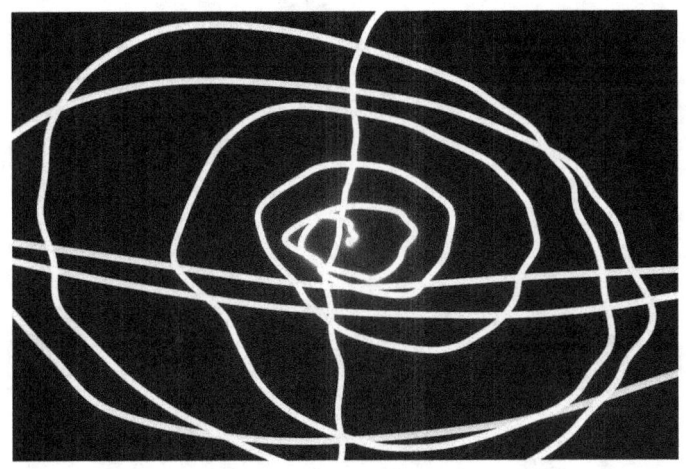

> *I name the moons, count the days,*
> *salute the sun when I awake,*
> *I found some friends along the way,*
> *we ride the seasons and celebrate…*

**It is helpful to track key lunar and solar events as they are auspicious times for prayers, ceremonies, and other activities.** Your actions on these days will be amplified by the natural powers inherent in them. You can mark these power days on your calendar and use them to schedule ceremonies, Nature retreats, days off, and other important activities so that you can benefit more deeply from them.

Find data at: www.timeanddate.com/astronomy

180　Inquire Within

# *Appendix Two*
# Book, Web, Music & Movie Resources

*I Am That I Am.*

These books, websites, albums, and movies were created by visionaries, sages, and scholars - experts in their fields. These world-class offerings will allow you to research and explore the subjects covered in this book in much more detail.

# Book Resources

Barrios, Carlos (2010). ***The Book of Destiny:*** *Unlocking the Secrets of the Ancient Mayans and the Prophecy of 2012.* HarperOne. Translated from the Spanish by Lisa Carter. *(Written at the request of the Mayan elders by a Mayan priest, the book is a tool to help people understand their life purpose and use this knowledge to make the best of their time on Earth)*

Campbell, Joseph with Bill Moyers (1988). ***The Power of Myth.*** Doubleday. *(Conversations about mythology and archetypes)*

Christopher, David (2004). ***The Holy Universe.*** New Story Press. *(A new story of creation for the heart, soul, and spirit)*

Chapman, Gary (1992). ***The 5 Love Languages:*** *The Secret to Love That Lasts.* Northfield Publishing. *(Simple and transformative ideas about lasting love)*

Chuen, Master Lam Kam (1998). ***The Personal Feng Shui Manual:*** *How to Develop a Healthy and Harmonious Lifestyle.* Henry Holt and Company *(A guide on how to employ the ancient Chinese wisdom of Feng Shui with your own personal characteristics in mind)*

Coelho, Paulo (1993). ***The Alchemist.*** HarperCollins Publishers. *(A fable about listening to your heart and following your dreams)*

Dass, Ram (1971). ***Be Here Now.*** Hanuman Foundation. *(Describes principles of transformation and living a sacred life)*

Dass, Ram (1977). ***Grist For The Mill.*** Bantam Books. *(A New Age classic discussing reality, personal growth, liberation, the nature of God, and more)*

Emmons Ph.D., Robert A. (2007). ***Thanks!*** *How Practicing Gratitude Can Make You Happier.* Houghton Mifflin *(A guide to putting the powerfully beneficial practice of gratitude to work in our life)*

Emoto, Masaru (2001). ***The Hidden Messages In Water.*** Atria Books. *(An exploration of water's susceptibility to human words and emotions, keeping in mind that humans are essentially water)*

Farmer, Steve (2002). ***Sacred Ceremony****: How to Create Ceremonies for Healing, Transitions, and Celebrations.* Hay House. *(How to create your own ceremonies to consecrate the critical events and passages on your life journey)*

Gibran, Kahil (1923). ***The Prophet.*** Alfred A. Knopf *(An inspiring and timeless collection of poetic vignettes illuminating the human heart and mind)*

Gray, Martin (2007). ***Sacred Earth****: Places of Peace and Power.* Sterling Publishing Co., Inc. *(A pilgrimage with pictures and commentary exploring sacred sites from all around the world)*

Grey, Alex (1998). ***The Mission of Art.*** Shambhala Publications, Inc. *(Advocates art as a revelatory and healing force)*

Hay, Louise (1999). ***You Can Heal Your Life.*** Hay House. *(Thought patterns for overcoming illness)*

HH Dalai Lama & Howard C. Cutler (1998). ***The Art of Happiness****: A Handbook for Living.* Hodder & Stoughton. *(His Holiness the Dalai Lama talks about how to find inner peace and happiness)*

Highland, Chris (2001) Editor. ***Meditations of John Muir****: Nature's Temple.* Wilderness Press. *(John Muir's musings on discovering God in nature)*

Krishnamurti, Jiddu (1989)**.** ***Think on These Things.*** Harper One. *(Penetrating and profound observations on modern life)*

Levine, Stephen (1979). ***A Gradual Awakening***. Anchor Books. *(A gentle introduction to meditation and an inspiring book for anyone interested in deep personal growth)*

Linn, Denise (1999). ***Altars:*** *Bringing Sacred Shrines Into Your Everyday Life*. Wellspring/Ballantine. *(Instruction and inspiration for integrating altars into your daily life)*

Lushwala, Arkan (2017). ***Deer & Thunder****: Indigenous Ways of Restoring the World*.

Lushwala, Arkan (2012). ***The Time of the Black Jaguar****: An offering of indigenous wisdom for the continuity of life on Earth*.

Malchiodi, Cathy A. (2002). ***The Soul's Palette: Drawing on Art's Transformative Powers.*** Shambhala Publications. *(A guide to using artistic process as a form of holistic healing)*

McTaggart, Lynne (2010). ***The Bond***: How to Fix Your Falling-Down World. *(A visionary plan for living in harmony with our true nature)*

Nanh, Thich Nat, and Larry Dossey (2006). ***The Energy of Prayer****: How to Deepen Your Spiritual Practice*. Parallax Press. *(Presents meditative prayer as a practice that helps anyone create healthy lives)*

Papp, James K. (2021). ***Deer, Tree, the Shaman, and the Sun****: A Story About Learning to Be Ourselves in a New World*. Planet Papp. *(A short story about the wild times of 2020 in the context of a long arc, anchored in our indigenous past and tracing forward to a harmonious future)*

Pennick, Nigel (1992). ***The Pagan Book of Days****: A Guide to the Festivals, Traditions, and Sacred Days of the Year*. Destiny Books. *(Solar, lunar, and other holidays from the perspective of Celtic, Roman, Egyptian, and other traditions)*

Pollan, Michael (1997). *The Omnivore's Dilemma*: A Natural History of Four Meals. Penguin. *(Where our food comes from and why it matters)*

Rogers, Carole Garibaldi (2004). *Fasting*: Exploring a Great Spiritual Practice. Ave Maria Press *(Explores the wisdom of fasting as well as the seasons and reasons for doing so)*

Ruiz, Don Miguel (1997). *The Four Agreements*: A Practical Guide to Personal Freedom. Amber-Allen Publishing, Inc. *(Toltec wisdom to help overcome self-limiting beliefs)*

Ryan, M.J. (1999). *Attitudes of Gratitude*: How to Give and Receive Joy Everyday of Your Life. Conari Press. *(Inspiration and support for cultivating gratitude)*

Sams, Jamie and David Carson (1997). *Medicine Cards*: The Power of Discovery Through the Ways of Animals. St. Martin's Press *(A simple, beautiful, and powerful divination tool)*

Silva, Freddy (2012). *The Divine Blueprint*: Temples, Power Places and the Global Plan to Shape the Human Soul. Invisible Temple. *(A fresh and insightful account of the role played by sacred sites in raising human consciousness)*

Tolle, Eckhart (2004). *The Power of Now*: A Guide to Spiritual Enlightenment. Namaste Publishing *(A guide to spiritual awakening)*

Villoldo, Ph.D., Alberto (2006). *The Four Insights*: Wisdom, Power, and Grace of the Earthkeepers. Hay House. *(Wisdom teachings of the medicine men and women of the Americas for healing and spiritual evolution)*

Villoldo, Ph.D., Alberto (2015). *One Spirit Medicine*: Ancient Ways to Ultimate Wellness. Hay House. *(A guide drawing on ancient principles and practices for healing in all aspects of life)*

Watts, Alan (1989). ***The Book****: On the Taboo Against Knowing Who You are*. Vintage Books (reissue). *(A mind-opening exploration into personal identity and what it means to be human)*

Weil M.D., Andrew (2001). ***Eating Well For Optimum Health****: The Essential Guide to Bringing Health and Pleasure Back to Eating*. Collins Living. *(Healthy recommendations for food, nutrition, diet, and health)*

Wesselman Ph.D., Hank (2011). ***The Bowl of Light****: Ancestral Wisdom from a Hawaiian Shaman*. Sounds True, Inc. *(Powerful and inspiring teachings from the ancient Polynesian culture)*

William, Anthony (2015). ***Medical Medium:*** *Secrets Behind Chronic and Mystery Illness and How to Finally Heal*. Hay House.

Williamson, Marianne (2006). ***The Gift of Change***. HarperOne. *(Empowerment to see life's transitions as opportunities for growth and rebirth)*

Yogananda, Paramahansa (1946). ***Autobiography of a Yogi***. Self-Realization Fellowship. *(Fabulous stories from the life of this legendary spiritual teacher and an engaging introduction to the science of yoga and meditation)*

Yogananda, Parahahansa (1997). ***Journey to Self-Realization:*** *Discovering the Gifts of the Soul*. Self-Realization Fellowship. *(Collected talks and essays on living a spiritual life and experiencing the Divine Presence within)*

Yutang, Lin (1948). ***The Wisdom of Laotse***. The Modern Library. *(A beautiful translation of, and introduction, to Lao Tzu's classic "Tao Te Ching")*

# Web Resources

***Chicken Soup for the Soul.*** Jack Canfield and Mark Victor Hansen.
   www.chickensoup.com
   *(Stories bringing hope, courage, inspiration and love)*

***Creativity Portal***
   www.creativity-portal.com
   *(Resources inspiring creative exploration and expression)*

***Fun With Qigong – Qigong Training.*** Robert Bates
   www.funwithqigong.com
   *(Easy, gentle exercises for optimal health)*

***Gratefulness.org***
   www.gratefulness.org
   *(Resources for living in the gentle power of gratefulness)*

***Greater Good Science Center***
   greatergood.berkeley.edu
   *(The science of a meaningful life: compassion, gratitude, happiness, and more)*

***Hay House Radio***
   www.hayhouseradio.com
   *(Radio shows from some of the world's greatest teachers in spirituality, health, and wellness)*

***The Holy Universe.*** David Christopher.
   www.theseekerandthesage.com
   *(Inspiration to find your path in the midst of turbulent times)*

***How to Meditate.***
   www.how-to-meditate.org
   *(Practical information on why and how to practice meditation)*

*Light of Consciousness.* Swami Amar Jyoti.
   www.light-of-consciousness.org
   (*Spiritual inspiration for all faiths and religions*)

*Mayan Calendar Portal.*
   www.maya-portal.net
   (*A Mayan Calendar community*)

*Radical Forgiveness - Finding Peace, Love & Acceptance.*
   www.radicalforgiveness.com
   (*Whatever your problem, Radical Forgiveness is the answer*)

*Rob Schouten Gallery.* Visionary/Spiritual Art.
   www.robschoutengallery.com
   (*Soulful images of harmony and beauty, like this book cover*)

*Saq' Be' Organization for Mayan and Indigenous Spiritual Studies*
   www.sacredroad.org

*Spiritual Media Blog.* Dr. Matthew Welsh J.D., Ph.D.
   www.spiritualitymediablog.com
   (*Psychology, spirituality, and inspirational entertainment*)

*Spirituality and Practice.* Resources for spiritual journeys.
   www.spiritualityandpractice.com

*The Spirit of Now – Three Minute Meditation.* Peter Russell.
   www.peterrussell.com/TV/3Min.php
   (*Short guided meditation*)

*TimeAndDate.com*
   https://www.timeanddate.com
   (*Sun, noon, equinox, solstice data, and more*)

*Yoga Journal.* Online retreat for yoga, classes, meditation, and life.
   www.yogajournal.com

# Music – Sound Resources

*Amber Sky* (2017). Dean Evenson, Phil Heaven, Jeff Willson. Soundings of the Planet. *(Flute, viola, and keyboards set a mood of calm and gratitude for the beauty all around us)*

*Ambient 2: The Plateaux of Mirror* (1980). Harold Budd and Brian Eno. E.G. Records. *(Dreamlike, timeless piano passages)*

*Apollo: Atmospheres and Soundtracks* (1990). Brian Eno with Daniel Lanois and Roger Eno. E.G. Records. *(Hauntingly gorgeous ambient music)*

*Atlantis Angelis* (1990). Patrick Bernard. MaGaDa HeRiTaGe Int'l. *(Soothing, calming passages of peace and tranquility)*

*Bliss* (1998). Various Artists. Real World. (A *hauntingly enchanting mix of beautiful world music)*

*Café del Mar Volume Once* (2004). Various Artists. Ibiza Spain. *(Chill-out music filled with wonder and light)*

*Chakra Suite* (2001). Steven Halpern. Inner Peace Music. *(Healing music for meditation and relaxation)*

*Crystal Sounds (Music for the Nature - Devas)* (2000). Rainier Tillman. Binkey Kok Publications. *(Crystal singing bowls vibrate as meditative jewels of sound)*

*Dance of Shakti* (2001). Prem Joshua. White Swan Music *(A divine tapestry of devotional trance music from India)*

*Deep Forest* (1992). Celine Music/Syncsound. *(Fusion of ambient techno with ethnic musicses)*

*Desert Vision* (1987). David Lanz & Paul Speer. Narada Productions. *(Music inspired by the land of the Southwest and dedicated to the Great Spirit of the Native American)*

***Discreet Music*** (1975). Brian Eno. E.G. Records. *(Minimalist ambient mood music)*

***Dreamtime Return*** (1988). Steve Roach. Soundquest Music/Fortuna One Music. *(A masterpiece of vastness and mystery inspired by Australian aboriginal mythology)*

***Medicine Woman*** (2001). Medwyn Goodall. New World Music. *(Nature inspired music celebrating the power of the feminine)*

***Mountain Meadow Meditation*** (2003). Dean Evenson & Scott Huckabay. Soundings of the Planet. *(Soothing songs of harmony featuring flute, guitar, sitar, harp, and more.)*

***Music for the Native Americans*** (1994). Robbie Robertson & The Red Road Ensemble. Capitol Records. *(Music written by Mr. Robertson and colleagues, inspired by his Mohawk heritage)*

***Mystic Spirit Voices*** (1999). Lesiem. Intencity Records. *(A journey through majestic spirit voices)*

***Nataraja*** (2006). Shiva Rea. Sounds True. *(Songs compiled from Shiva Rea's Yoga Trance Dance DVD)*

***Om Sanctuary*** (1998). J.D. McKean. JDM Music. *(The most sacred of universal tones is chanted, accompanied by harp and synthesizer)*

***Oxygène*** (1976). Jean-Michel Jarre. Disques Dreyfus/Polydor. *(Spacious, entrancing instrumental electronica that takes you on a journey)*

***Planetary Unfolding*** (1981). Michael Stearns. Continuum Montage - Sonic Atmospheres. *(An ambient music classic that elegantly and unhurriedly intimates a world made of sound)*

***Red Moon*** (2003). Peter Kater. Silver Wave. *(An ensemble collection of haunting melodies with a Native American inflection)*

***Sacred Earth Drums*** (1994). David and Steve Gordon. Sequoia Records. *(Shamanic drumming that leads you on a healing journey)*

***Shaman*** (2000). Troika. Enso Records. *(Travel to new dimensions and the mystical, powerful world of spirit healers)*

***Shamanic Dream II*** (2002). Anguma. Open Sky Music. *(Relaxing and gentle trance meditation music)*

***Shaman's Eye*** (2007). Liquid Bloom. White Swan Records. *(Healing rhythms for trance meditation)*

***Shiva Moon*** (2005). Prem Joshua. Spice Records. *(A heavenly fusion of classical Indian music with trance music)*

***Wind Songs*** (1996). Michael Hoppe' & Tim Wheater. Spring Hill Music. *(Beautiful, expansive flute improvisations of incredible depth)*

## Movies – Audio-Visual Resources

*10 Questions For The Dalai Lama* (2006). Rick Ray. Rick Ray Films. *(The Dalai Lama responds to questions concerning non-violence, happiness, and other fundamental questions of our time)*

*Avatar* (2009). James Cameron. Fox.
*(A movie about the connections of humans to each other and to the Earth)*

*Awake: The Life of Yogananda* (2014). Lisa Leeman, Paola di Florio. CounterPoint Films. *(A biopic about Paramahansa Yogananda, spiritual teacher and author of Autobiography of a Yogi)*

*The Connected Universe* (2016). Malcom Carter. Chronos Global Media Inc. *(Explores the science behind the interconnection of all things in the universe)*

*Conversations With God* (2007). Stephen Deutsch. CWG Productions. *(A dramatic, true, inspiring story of a struggling man who battles homelessness and, with grace, turns his life around)*

*The Earthing Movie* (2019). Joshua Tickell, Rebecca Harrell Tickell. Big Picture Ranch, Gaia. *(A documentary about the profoundly healing effects of being barefoot on the Earth)*

*Fabulous Fungi* (2019). Louis Schwartzberg. Moving Art Studio, Reconsider. *(A time-lapse journey about the medicinal world of fungi and their power to heal - personally and planetarily)*

*Gandhi* (1982). Richard Attenborough. Columbia Pictures Corporation *(A film about Mohandas (Mahatma) Gandhi which illustrates the principle of non-violent non-cooperation)*

*Happy* (2011). Roko Belic. Emotion Content, Iris Films, Wadi Rum Films. *(Real life stories and powerful interviews explore what really makes people happy)*

*I Am* (2010). Tom Shadyac. Shady Acres Entertainment *(Intellectual and spiritual leaders talk about what is wrong with the world and how we can improve the way we live in it)*

*Inner World, Outer World* (2012). Daniel Schmidt. New Media Film Festival. *(Examines the vibratory source that connections all things and links our inner and outer worlds)*

*It's a Wonderful Life* (1946). Frank Capra. Prime Time Productions. *(Shows us that, despite our problems, we really do have "a wonderful life")*

*Life in a Day* (2011). Loressa Clisby and Kevin Macdonald. LG, Scott Free Productions, YouTube. *(Footage from all over the world on 24 July 2010 shows what it means to be human in the world today)*

*The Need to Grow* (2019). Rob Herring and Ryan Wirick. 4WT Media and Earth Conscious Films. *(A food documentary which offers hope and solutions in a dire time for our planet and civilization)*

*Peaceful Warrior* (2004). Victor Salva. Universal Studios. *(An unlikely spiritual journey with a powerful and timeless message about how to approach life's challenges)*

*People vs. The State of Illusion* (2012). Scott Corvine, Austin Vickers. Exalt Films, Movies From The Heart. *(A compelling docudrama explores the science and power of perception and imagination)*

*Planet Earth* (2007). BBC Worldwide. *(An incomparable view of the awesome beauty and diversity of the natural world)*

***Ram Dass, Fierce Grace*** (2001). Mickey Lemie. Lemie Pictures. *(Spiritual inspiration and meditation on spirituality, consciousness, healing, and grace)*

***Samsara*** (2011). Ron Fricke. Freestyle Digital Media. *(Beautifully filmed over 5 years in 25 countries, Samsara takes us to sacred grounds, disaster zones, and natural wonders)*

***The Secret*** (2006). Drew Heriot and Sean Byrne. Prime Time Productions. *(Explores the law of attraction - the secret to prosperity, health, relationships, and happiness)*

***The Shift*** (2009). Michael Goorjian. Lyceum Films. *(A dramatic and compelling exploration of the journey from ambition to meaning)*

***Spiritual Revolution*** (2008). Alan Sawyer. East Meets West Productions. *(Explores the very real power of meditation)*

***Waking Life*** (2001). Richard Linklater. Fox Searchlight Pictures. *(A man tries to figure out if he is living in reality or just dreaming in this animated philosophical exploration)*

***What the Bleep Do We Know!?*** (2004). Betsy Chasse, Mark Vicente, William Arntz. 20th Century Fox. *(Interviews, drama, and special effects combine to illustrate the power and value of positive thinking)*

***Wings of Desire*** (1988). Wim Wenders. Road Movies Filmproduktion. *(Explores the longing for and love of life)*

# Afterword – A Prayer

*May each of us on this Earth
be blessed to feel the Love in our heart*

*And may each of us on this Earth
be blessed to open our heart*

*And may the Love in our heart
shine out into the world,
casting its glow upon all*

*And by this glow may we recognize
each other as Solar Brothers and Sisters,
children of the same family
of Father Sun and Mother Earth*

*And may Peace prevail.*

## 196 Inquire Within

# Biography

James K. Papp was born and raised in Fairbanks, Alaska. He first kept a journal when he was a child. Here is an entry made when he was age six:

James has spent over four decades studying metaphysics and spirituality. His education includes learning and practice with Mayan spiritual teachers and a shaman in the Q'ero Andean tradition. James is a loving husband, a successful CEO, and an award-winning landscape photographer whose work is featured internationally. He is also the author of *Deer, Tree, the Shaman, and the Sun: A Story About Learning to Be Ourselves in a New World*. He resides in Washington State with his wife Lisa.

*Namasté*

www.ingramcontent.com/pod-product-compliance
Lightning Source LLC
Chambersburg PA
CBHW071918290426
44110CB00013B/1403